American Conservatism Truth Versus The Cognitive Dissonance Of Liberal Thinking

Michael J. Broch

ISBN-13: 978-1490443843
ISBN-10: 1490443843

DEDICATION

We all owe in some measure the very essence of whom and what we are to other great people in our lives. Those people not only supported us, they influenced us, helped shaped our thinking and walked with us, sometimes leading and sometimes watchfully following, along the path of life to where we are today.

I would like to dedicate what I have written here to my wife of 40 years, Debbie. We met at age 19 and were married soon after, when I returned from "My Beginnings". While the Liberals in my family disparage me most for my views, I was the one who was a young Liberal and who was clueless, whereas Debbie believed in the teachings of Ayn Rand and was the Conservative thinker in the family. Without her guidance, love and support, the cloud of Liberalism that hung over me when I was young might never have lifted; and, if not, I might still be one of the Liberals I disdain most and argue against herein.

Without the love and guidance of my wife, Debbie, I would not have learned the lessons I have about personal responsibility and I certainly would not have experienced the joy and life lessons that have come from having kids and grandkids. And, without Debbie's unbounded kindness and support, I would not be the same person who I am so proud of being today; and that is a husband, a father, a grandfather and a patriotic Conservative American.

COVER – EXPLANATION

I have been asked, what is your cover illustration meant to represent? The lady is Astraea, who is known as a goddess of justice from Greek mythology and who is thought to be either the daughter of Themis and Zeus or of Eos and Astraeus. This symbol, of Astraea, or the Blind Lady of Justice, is an important foundation of American jurisprudence, in that justice is or should be blind to all except the facts. In the cover illustration, the scale of justice is heavily weighted towards Conservatism designated in red (vis-à-vis red vs. blue states), based on the facts presented herein that Conservatism is far more just than is the cognitive dissonance of Liberalism and Liberal thinking.

CONTENTS

1 PROLOGUE – THE AGE OF ENLIGHTENMENT AND MY BEGINNINGS

The times were the late 1960's and early 1970's. At least for those of us involved in the movement, this was the "Age of Enlightenment", of a true Renaissance. Not only were we the enlightened, we felt indeed that we were the first generation ever to realize that the world needed to be changed, transformed, perhaps even in a direction that we did not yet clearly see, but change was needed. We also knew that the status quo, the establishment as it was, was no longer acceptable, or fair, or just and that the responsibility for needed social change was ours and ours alone. For we were the first generation of outspoken Liberal radicals – others called us "hippies" – but we just thought of ourselves as "far out", smarter, and more enlightened than everyone else.

In protest from the nation's college campuses, to its streets and to Woodstock, from mostly young to some old, including most if not all of the left leaning college professors who also wanted to be seen as enlightened, we gathered, grew in numbers and marked ourselves as being separate from the rest of society, by our long hair for men, pants for women and patchouli oil and drugs. We first started the foundation of social change by blurring the line between the sexes, because after all were we not all equal, all part of the same collective, and therefore no one person should stand above the others, or appear differently, or be socially more advantaged, or wealthier? And so, women wore their hair short and looked like men, men emulated women and everyone wore the same perfume. And most of all, we protested against the rest of society - the establishment - because society as structured was flawed and evil.

What we believed in most and championed hardest was equality for all, meaning sameness in social treatment, whether black or white, man or woman, young or old. Of course this equality really only pertained to those of us who were enlightened. It certainly was not extended to the military, or to anyone in the perceived establishment, or especially to the police, for obvious reasons. Furthermore, it did not apply to anyone who was religious or deemed "Conservative". Conservatism was, after all, the foundation and the epitome of the establishment. Conservatives were the sworn enemies, for they were the true enemies of social change and enlightenment. Clearly incapable of enlightenment, these people were red necks, fundamentally different from us, not only not to be trusted but to be outright hated.

It was an amazing and wonderful time for us, for we were the messiahs, the anointed ones, even if admittedly self-anointed, and we were smarter, more enlightened and simply more far out than any generation that there had ever been before us, or probably would ever come after us. To prove how enlightened we were, we read Marx, Engels, Mein Kampf and the I Ching, and we discussed and meditated on the yin and the yang, on Confucius and on spiritual enlightenment. We abhorred any war, especially the one in Vietnam. After all, what right did we have to impose their beliefs on others? Communism certainly was not bad. We revered as our own heroes Che Guevara and Fidel Castro. The problem wasn't communism - the problem was capitalism. The real social problem was the chains that Capitalism placed on the people, us the proletariat, by the evil corporations that were forcing us into essential slavery. This slavery after all was imposed on us by corporations that were structured to do only one thing and that was to make money and by doing so to promote the two concepts we hated most - social inequality and the creation and promotion of the "haves" through corporate profits and greed. We of course were the "have not's", but we were also part of society and thus we believed that we were entitled to all of its fruits, rather than the riches being hoarded by a few selfish undeserving and unenlightened individuals.

To promote our radicalism we marched in active protests across the nation and we especially strongly opposed the Vietnam War. We asked, "What was wrong with the United States government and by extension the military and the men who served in the military? How could they not see that the war was unjust and unnecessary? At times we actually hoped for defeat in the war, and we hated anything to do with the military, because it was indeed the sum of all bad things – an evil entity created by white Conservatives to pursue the goals of the establishment by bringing the horrors of war and death to the world's innocents. And when Saigon fell in 1975, many of us outwardly rejoiced and actively denigrated our military men as they returned defeated from the war. After all, this was a war we were against from the beginning; we had marched against it, we had regaled against it at every opportunity and unlike others we knew we had right on our side - because this war was the epitome of evil itself, only created by men who saw evil in communism, where no evil truly existed.

And so our enlightenment grew even more. And what we primarily stood "for" was to be "against". We were against most ideas rather than being for them. You had to be against and hate all corporations, especially big oil, big pharmaceutical companies, big car manufacturers, tobacco companies, Wall Street, the banks and the rich. We were against all wars, against most government and against capitalism. We certainly were not for the Constitution of the United States, except certain clauses like "… all men are created equal…", because that document clearly was written by old white men who had no concept at all of what a modern free society should really be.

But, we were "for" some ideals. We were of course for Unions, because they represented the struggle of the proletariat against the bourgeoisie. We were for all of the country's disenfranchised people, including American Indians and Blacks, because they had suffered mightily at the hands of the white capitalists and racists. And, we were for America in concept, but of course not the America of the present, but rather the America of our perceived future making - the way it would be under our plan; a plan of hope and change, but not one tied down to the impediments of either a real outline or a real platform. After all, we were free thinkers and, as such, free thinkers evolve and should not be forced to fully codify their beliefs of the moment or to be tied down to concepts that may well change as new visions or new enlightenments arose.

As a group, we were certainly for the redistribution of wealth. After all, why should some people have more money than others? Shouldn't they give freely of their labor or, if not, to have that money forcibly taken from them by the government for the benefit of the less fortunate? We believed in a communal society. And being part of a commune meant that we should all share equally. Russia had the right idea. Maybe Communism as a government was a little harsh, but socialism as an economic principle done in a new way under America's newly enlightened visionaries, us, would be the answer to all of the world's suffering and pain.

Another important concept that we were for was "not having to work". Why should anyone be forced to spend their life toiling for money when they could spend their time on this earth doing as they pleased, whether they were involved in art, entertainment, sex, drugs or anything they wanted to do or to be at the moment? We applauded Europe and its high youth unemployment rates and socialized societies. Europe's youth did not have to work, why should we?

And, perhaps most importantly, we were for environmentalism. After all, rich people were responsible for senselessly polluting and destroying the planet. Why should some live in big houses and own fancy cars, clearly at an enormous expense to the environment, when we could all live communally, with nature instead of against it? We were especially happy when DDT was found in peregrine falcon eggs in Alaska and was banned from use in the US in 1972 and soon afterward worldwide by the UN. It was finally time for society to recognize and do something about the capitalistic chemical companies that were destroying our environment in the quest of a few meaningless dollars. And after all, the media had been telling us since the 1950's that human activities on this planet were leading to catastrophic global cooling and the beginning of a new Ice Age, and those alarms had grown even more strident recently.

In spite of all of these challenges, we felt that we were alone on the path of attaining true Nirvana – a Utopian society where we were all equal and in being equal would all be truly happy. And in that Nirvana, rules would not be needed, nor should they exist, and thus the rules of the present world should not be applied to us at all. We were above those rules and beyond being fettered by the mundane bonds of a society, or by individuals in that society who did not understand our goals or dreams. We believed that we had the freedom and thus the right to do whatever we wanted, whenever we wanted to do it, as long as it was acceptable within our own Liberal culture. So when we marched and got arrested we did not care. And those bold transgressions became a badge of honor – to have taken on the police and the establishment and to have walked away with no real consequences. That was, well, far out – to be respected. What about the potential downside of having a criminal record? Since there were no records in our world, the criminal record of the establishment world was meaningless and held no sway over us and we embraced it like a badge of honor.

In our struggle for true equality for all, we were especially and universally against all racism. I laugh even today at people who know nothing of history who think they are the first individuals or the first generation to abhor racism. They have no idea of what we were up against and how we stood up to it. How many people today have been were willing to be involved in a fight, because a redneck said in their presence, "the only good nigger is a dead nigger?" [Note that I use these words for accuracy and to give factual weight to the anger I felt on hearing them.] I have and I won that argument more than once on the basis of right and righteous anger on my side. As a group, we believed that racism was bad and that meant any racism, including reverse racism. The absurd notion that only white people can be racist, held by some today, was not conceivable to us at that time. But, after all, we were purists and we were smarter, and we knew for certain that if racism is wrong, which it is, then all racism is bad and racism cannot be tolerated in any society that considers itself enlightened.

Politically we recognized that we had a problem. After all, if you are truly against all of society's foundations, as a purist you really can't support government in any form. And so for the most part we did not support America's political foundations. We did this simply by not voting. However, most of us felt that the party with the only real affinity to us was the Democrat party. After all, weren't the Democrats for the common man, and weren't they the party of the Unions and the proletariat? Republicans of course were universally bad. The Republicans were, 1) Conservative, 2) religious, and 3) supportive of big business and corporations. All of this amounted to three fatal strikes. None of us, the enlightened, would ever admit to being a Republican, nor would he or she ever outwardly support any Republican candidate or concept.

However, we also knew that the Democrats, particularly the southern Democrats, had been the ones opposed to civil rights for Blacks in the 1960's and earlier the Democrats had mostly been against women's suffrage. So by extension we all became "northern" Democrats. And, in doing so, we could finally support politically the arena of the blue collar worker and become political champions of the common man, all of which were fundamental pillars of our emerging new Liberal belief platform.

For President of the United States, we only supported those individuals whom we deemed to be radical. As a group and as a movement, we were indeed crushed in 1972 when George McGovern lost by a landslide to Richard Nixon. Clearly the rest of America did not understand, but that was no surprise to us, given the challenge of Mein Kampf, or "our struggle". But it taught us something about the need to vote for your beliefs, beyond simply to smoke dope and to talk about them.

And so against this backdrop, with long hair and $180 to my name, I dropped out of college, grabbed a coat and a sleeping bag and hitchhiked across America. It was truly sobering to be entirely alone and sleeping at night along the side of the road in the rain and humidity and covered with mosquitoes. Hassled by cops and rednecks, I found out what true prejudice really felt like for the first time, and my journey supported what I had already come to believe, that injustice truly existed throughout the world and throughout America.

After a while I met others like me in southern California and was invited to live in a commune in the hills overlooking the backside of Santa Barbara. In this commune we took off our clothes, bathed in streams and began the process of creating a true nirvana, our own Utopian world, with our own true believers.

Of course, the first requirement of joining a commune was to give up all your possessions. So, I bought six goats for the group with the entirety of my $180. The best part of this was, since I bought the goats I did not have to milk them – someone else did that. And so we settled into our self-made nirvana, safe and removed from the establishment and the rest of society. We ate berries and nuts, because clearly eating meat and hunting was bad, and we smoked pot, all the while contemplating true enlightenment, the meaning of life and the wonder of our own Utopia. And we were truly free from of all of society's bonds, because after all we were penniless.

For me Utopia lasted about two weeks. While going naked had its own kind of freedom, it didn't do much for me. Our stash of dried fruits and nuts was running out. And, who could ever like goat's milk? Our talk around the campfire was not awe inspiring either, because there was no future to discuss, and you can only say "far out" or "cool" a few hundred times a day before it starts to get boring. Having time to think, I realized that it was early fall, schools around the nation had already started and the world was moving forward - without me. I did not much like to smoke pot anyway, and I liked to fish and hunt. In fact most of the collective's Utopia did not seem to be my Utopia at all. Contrary to my first expectations, I was not truly happy in this Utopia and I was restless. And so, after a while it became time for me to move on…

And so, I sold my sleeping bag for $20, left the few things I owned behind and hitchhiked back to Pullman, Washington. Within four months I was married, was seeking a job and was making plans to return to college. Abruptly, my term as a hippie and as a left wing radical came to an end, as it did for most others. But what I and others did not know at that time was that the movement was not really dead at all. Rather, it was still living on, primarily in the halls of America's universities and in the minds of some radical individuals who never had to face the combined reality of a job, marriage and the responsibility of having children in the real world. These Liberal activists instead went into politics or into the universities, where they could be removed from reality. And they became the people who would take our 1960's and 1970's radicalism and turn it into a political platform, and then use it some 40 years later to destroy not only America and our own futures, but also our children's futures and the very foundations of our society.

You see, we never really believed, or at least most of us didn't, that what we proposed as a movement was ever realistically achievable. What we did and what we believed in was mostly done to protest against the war and the foundations of our parents, as every generation is wont to do. In retrospect our movement was about one thing and one thing only, and that was about the self - me, myself and I – the same as modern Liberalism today.

In a very short time of living in a commune and on the road, I had learned a very important life lesson. That lesson was that Sir Thomas Moore was right in 1516 when, while describing Utopia in the context of an ideally perfect place, he coined the term Utopia from the Greek: οὐ, "not", and τόπος, "place", or "not place", indicating that he was utilizing the concept as allegory and as such did not consider such an ideal place to be realistically possible. And why isn't a Utopia, or why aren't Utopian concepts, possible? It is because every man and women is happy under a different set of changing circumstances and conditions.

During the time of my sojourn to the Left, the federal budget moved from a $10 billion annual rate of surplus in the first half of calendar 1969 to an $18 billion deficit in the first half of 1972. In the early 1970s, inflation caused by rising prices for imported commodities, especially oil, and spending on the Vietnam War, which was not counteracted by cuts in other government expenditures, combined with a trade deficit to create a situation in which the dollar was worth less than the gold used to back it. And deaths worldwide, especially of children, skyrocketed into the millions due to huge increases in malaria cases after the banning of DDT.

According to Wikipedia, "*In 1971, President Richard Nixon unilaterally ordered the cancellation of the direct convertibility of the United States dollar to gold. This act was known as the Nixon Shock*". In 1972, the United States reset the value of one troy ounce of gold to 38 dollars. Because other currencies were valued in terms of the U.S. dollar, this failed to resolve the disequilibrium between the U.S. dollar and other currencies. As a consequence, in 1975 the United States began to float the dollar with respect to both gold and other currencies. With this new monetary policy, the US was for the first time fully on a fiat currency. And, the ultra-Liberals who simply did not exist in great numbers before the early 1970's grew older, ran for public office and began to take over America's universities, the Press and the government itself.

These circumstances set the stage for what we have today, loose fiscal policy, a diminished public moral foundation for the country and a federal government that is destroying America. While I slowly became more and more Conservative in my outlook, as I grew from the 1970's to the 1980's and beyond, during which time I travelled the world, built an economic foundation through education, hard work and effort, and learned to love my family and my country more and more every day, a degeneration of everything that I had grown to love and respect was occurring in America.

I feel that as a father, husband, grandfather and a part of a greater family of mankind that it is my responsibility to put in writing the things I have learned about the politics and direction of our country during my lifetime. I hope that I have set out what I have learned through the years in the following in a logical, well-reasoned approach that others can understand and hopefully learn from. I try to use extensively quotes from others, in part because they have said things better than I ever could, but also to place into proper historic context where Conservative ideals have truly come from, and they are from the great men and women who have gone before us.

For you people who classify yourselves as Liberals, what I have written may be painful for you to read and it may anger you. But, as you read this, many of you who think of yourselves as being Liberal may come to realize that you do not agree with the ideology of the Left and that you are actually Conservative in nature. Irrespective, at least read what I have written, because if nothing else I hope that you will understand what the other side, the Conservatives of America, really believe, because while Liberals vilify us every day for what they *think* we believe, I am certain that they have no idea what we really stand for, and especially what I have learned during my 40+ years of growth from being a clueless young Liberal to becoming a true patriotic Conservative American.

2 WHAT IS COGNITIVE DISSONANCE?

Fifty years ago (1957), social psychologist Leon Festinger published in his seminal analysis, A Theory of Cognitive Dissonance, the following observations, "*Persons are not always successful in explaining away or in rationalizing inconsistencies to themselves. For one reason or another, attempts to achieve consistency may fail. The inconsistency then simply continues to exist… When the dissonance is present, in addition to trying to reduce it, the person will actively avoid situations and information which would likely increase the dissonance.*" What this means is that, according to Wikipedia, "*The theory of cognitive dissonance in social psychology proposes that people have a motivational drive to reduce dissonance by altering existing cognitions, adding new ones to create a consistent belief system, or alternatively by reducing the importance of any one of the dissonant elements.*"

The following sections illustrate how Conservative beliefs are internally consistent, whereas to be a Liberal one must deal not only with a set of beliefs that are entirely conflicting, but they must deal with numerous true cognitive dissonances between what are rational or even cogent positions within their own belief system. This explains why most Liberals will not listen to any Conservative discussion, nor will they even read a book such as this, because they are always on the edge of uncontrollable hatred and anger verging on mental instability, due to the numerous cognitive dissonances contained within their own Liberal Pandora's Box of political beliefs. The Liberal collection of viewpoints and beliefs are indeed so dissonant that no other viewpoints can be tolerated at all, even to the extent of Liberals altering their own existing cognitions, so that they can better cope with the deafening dissonances of their own beliefs.

The back leaf of this book contains the following quote from me, which captures the reality of truth versus the cognitive dissonance of Liberal denial:

> *When brought to light, the truth of facts will banish political opinions back to the dark recesses of biased prejudices, except for those who refuse to see the light.*

3 LIBERAL VERSUS "PROGRESSIVE" AND THE DEFINITION OF CONSERVATISM

First, I would like to clarify why I use the term Liberal and not the word "progressive" throughout in the following to describe Liberalism in America. This is because, while the Liberals want to label themselves as progressives, there is nothing whatsoever that is progressive about their beliefs. The term progressive is defined in part as, "*of, relating to, or characterized by progress*" or "*making use of or interested in new ideas, findings, or opportunities*". The exact opposite is true about Liberalism in this country. The socialist ideas Liberals subscribe to have, for the most part, been tried in the past and have failed miserably, so these ideas cannot be considered either to be new or to be progressive in any form. Rather, today's progressives would be better described in terms of the lessons of history as truly being "regressives", both in terms of economics and social policies.

In the past, the term Liberal was used for someone who believed in liberty, but that is the last concept that most Liberals subscribe to today. More correctly, modern Liberals mostly believe in being liberal with other people's money.

I also use the term Conservative throughout this document, rather than the term Republican or on the Right. Conservatism is an ideology, whereas being a Republican is a political party affiliation. And, while many Republicans are Conservative and are on the right, too many are not Conservative and are rhinos or "Republicans in name only". I do not use the characterization of Right and Left as frequently herein, because these words speak little of the beliefs of either side and are frequently used by one side or another to pigeonhole the beliefs of others, oftentimes irrespective of reality. However, since the words Right and Left are of common and accepted usage, I do use them wherever I believe that it is appropriate to do so.

With regards to the definition of what a Conservative is, I agree most with a portion of Wikipedia's quote, as follows, " *According to [Lord] Hailsham, a former chairman of the British Conservative Party, "Conservatism is not so much a philosophy as an attitude, a constant force, performing a timeless function in the development of a free society, and corresponding to a deep and permanent requirement of human nature itself.*"

4 AN INTRODUCTION TO WHAT AMERICAN CONSERVATIVES BELIEVE

Liberals in America, and in fact most people around the world, either do not understand, or do not care to understand, what Conservatives in America actually stand for and believe in. American Conservatives are indeed unique, because we believe in doctrines and concepts found nowhere else in the world, and they are those that are codified in the Declaration of Independence and in the Constitution of the United States. These two documents enshrined into the nation, and into the nation's laws, the inimitable concepts of liberty, freedom and a government of the people, by the people, and for the people. "*We hold these truths to be self-evident, that all men are created equal, that they are endowed by their Creator with certain unalienable Rights, that among these are Life, Liberty and the pursuit of Happiness-- That to secure these rights, Governments are instituted among Men, deriving their just powers from the consent of the governed...*" Inherent in these founding principles is that rights are not conferred by men, but rather they are inherited from a higher authority, they are inalienable and thus they are more fundamental and overarching than the laws created by man, whatever each individual's concept of a Creator may be. Also intrinsic to these founding principles are the concepts of self-determination, of limited government and of a representative republic, rather than a true democracy, because according to Thomas Jefferson "*A democracy is nothing more than mob rule, where fifty-one percent of the people may take away the rights of the other forty-nine*".

Unlike Liberalism, American Conservatism is based on principles, ideas and concepts that require rational thought and examination to fully understand and to appreciate. And, as such, they are not based on emotion, nor are they based on what has been aptly described for Liberal thinking as true cognitive dissonance or "invincible ignorance coupled with mind numbing hypocrisy".

American Conservatism is the antithesis of socialism, statism and autocratic rule and stands in diametric opposition to those beliefs. While American Conservatives believe that all people are created equal and thus deserve equal opportunity, we do not believe that anywhere inherent in these precepts is the concept of equal outcomes – the outcome is based on the individual, on their desire to contribute to society through their own abilities, effort and self-determination, as compared to the Liberal push towards collectivism, group thinking and dependency.

Conservatives believe that dependency destroys free will and by extension that it destroys individuals and societies. We believe that, while a giving and generous society is willing to give to others less fortunate a hand up, that giving them a never-ending handout is a certain recipe for illiteracy, dependency and the loss of personal determination and free will and thus a loss of personal freedom – a precious freedom that each and every one of us is sworn to protect, both for ourselves and for all of mankind.

Conservatives strongly believe that all men are created equal with the inalienable rights to life, liberty and the pursuit of happiness, but it is important to understand that these are hierarchical rights, meaning that the right to life is first and most essential, followed by liberty and then by the pursuit of happiness, all of which are also reflected in the inherent right to one's own property. And these rights, being inalienable, cannot be taken from us the people either by other men or by government. And, since life in the first fundamental requirement for all other rights and all values, any "right" that violates that or any of the other rights in succession is in direct conflict with our inalienable rights and are not truly rights at all.

By extension of those inalienable rights, we Conservatives believe, as stated by Dean Kalahar, that "*…a person has a right, based on natural law, to their person and their possessions, and if property is generated by the productive and wealth creating behavior of a person's labor, then it follows that it is an infringement on an individual's rights to use any force (murder, theft, rape, etc.) to injure or take away one's property. Using the productivity of another for one's personal gain is immoral.*" Further, "*If taking the productive output of a slave and using it for another's personal gain is immoral; then taking the productive output of any worker and using it for another's gain is also immoral, no matter what race, color, gender, or socio-economic status the producer happens to be.*

As a result of believing that a person has a right to their own possessions and labor, Conservatives do not believe in the Liberal concepts of "economic fairness", "social justice", "economic justice," or "economic rights", because as stated by Kalahar, "*Logic leads us to one conclusion. A modern form of slavery has been embedded within the welfare state. And no matter how you slice it, property theft to promote a false ideology of "fairness" or advance a twisted form of "compassion" to gain power is abhorrent. It does not matter how many ribbons and bows decorate the rhetoric of "Robin Hood" redistribution, the final analysis is the promotion of servitude*". Also, as was stated by Bertrand de Jouvenel, "*The more one considers the matter, the clearer it becomes that redistribution is in effect far less a redistribution of free income from the richer to the poorer, as we imagined, than a redistribution of power from the individual to the State*".

We also believe, as stated by Kalahar, that "*Redistributive ideology is not about a safety net for the truly needy or the necessity of government to tax in order to perform its proper functions of protecting people, property, and enforcing the rule of law. President Obama may call it redistributive efforts," but in the end, using the power of the state to confiscate property is as immoral as taking the wealth created by a slave to benefit the slave owner*". And, as stated by Thomas Jefferson "*To take from one because it is thought that his own industry and that of his father's has acquired too much, in order to spare to others, who, or whose fathers, have not exercised equal industry and skill, is to violate arbitrarily the first principle of association -- the guarantee to every one of a free exercise of his industry and the fruits acquired by it*".

By extension to the above, Conservatives believe very strongly that free market capitalism is just, fair and moral, because it has led to less poverty, a higher standard of living and to true social and economic opportunity for people around the world, whereas socialism in direct contradiction is not only unfair, it is unjust and immoral, because where socialism has been tried it has resulted almost universally in higher rates of poverty, lower standards of living and in undeniable human misery, including even mass starvation and genocide. And, to simply ignore that socialism is immoral by treating it as both legal and acceptable because it is being forced on the people under the guise of government "largesse", or through a twisted sense of "fairness", is simply to not understand economics and economic outcomes, but it is also to willfully ignore what the very fundamentals of fairness, justice and morality truly stand for and mean.

Conservatives remember that America was founded by formerly repressed emigrants who wanted to establish a new country – a country in which all of its citizens would be free to believe as they wished, to speak and write as they desired, to go where they wanted and to pursue their lives and happiness as freely as possible. And, these people understood implicitly, as a result of their backgrounds and their knowledge of histories' lessons, that only government has the unstoppable power to suppress the people's liberty, by legally even using the forces of imprisonment and even death. As a result, they understood that the power of government must be limited and thus they created a new federal government – but one with extremely limited powers over the people. Inexplicably, Liberals do not understand this, that this great country became successful not as a result of government, but because the common people had the freedom to associate, to innovate, to take risk and to support each other both economically and socially. Liberals instead believe in an essentially unlimited government, with all of its deadly powers of coercion and even death over the people.

In particular, Conservatives believe that the ideals set out in the Constitution are timeless – that they are applicable today and will continue to be relevant long into the future, in direct contrast to Liberals, who not only do not believe in the Constitution but even worse demonize those who do.

Other major differences between Conservative and the cognitive dissonance of Liberal thinking in America are outlined below by topic, but are not set out in any particular order of relevance.

5 THE CONSTITUTION AND THE BILL OF RIGHTS

At the very core of Conservative beliefs and principles are an understanding of and an appreciation and support for, the United States Constitution in its entirety. Conservatives believe strongly in the ultimate reason for the creation of the Constitution, which was the establishment of the federal government by the people with certain enumerated powers solely for their safety and national security, or as described by John Adams, "*Government is instituted for the common good; for the protection, safety, prosperity, and happiness of the people; and not for profit, honor, or private interest of any one man, family, or class of men…*" And, Conservatives also strongly believe in the Bill of Rights, because our founding fathers understood that all governments can be corrupted by power, and, as best stated by Thomas Jefferson, "*A Bill of Rights is what the people are entitled to against every government, and what no just government should refuse, or rest on inference.*" When asked what the Bill of Rights is really about, very few Liberals will correctly answer that it is about defining the rights of the people against the government, as opposed to the rights of the federal government to control the people, and that it is the first 10 Amendments to the Constitution.

In direct contrast to Conservatives, Liberals in America constantly talk about how the Constitution is somehow outdated - that it was developed by old white guys, long dead and how it should be "a living and breathing" document. However, by doing so, Liberals want to ignore the Constitution of the United States to fit their ever evolving re-interpretation of what is important in government, because nowhere in the Constitution, which is indeed the ultimate law of the land, can there be found any legal basis for most of the Liberal perversions that include for example, the "right" to an abortion, healthcare, freedom "from" religion, a separation of church and state, the right to privacy (except the right against unreasonable search and seizure), federalism as opposed to the rights of the states, the taking of the fortune from one for the benevolence of another, a federal government with unlimited power and the Liberal irrational stance against the right to keep and bear arms.

Especially with regards to federal power, Liberals do not believe in and entirely ignore the Enumerated Powers Act, which is outlined in Article 1, Section 8 of the Constitution. This section outlines the entire legal scope of the federal government by ceding to the federal government only 17 enumerated powers, with all other powers reserved to the states and to the people, because "*these powers are delegated from the people and are the only Legislative*

Powers Congress has". But, our Founding Fathers went further, trying very diligently to make sure that the enumerated powers were so clear and so well defined that everyone in America could understand them. So, to further strengthen and clarify the enumerated powers of the federal government, and to further shut the door to claims of additional power by the same government, they passed the Ninth and Tenth Amendments. The Ninth Amendment states, "*The enumeration in the Constitution, of certain rights, shall not be construed to deny or disparage others retained by the people*". The Tenth Amendment states, "*The powers not delegated to the United States by the Constitution, nor prohibited by it to the States, are reserved to the States respectively, or to the people*".

Liberals ignore the supreme law of the land, the Constitution, but worse yet they never try to change it legally, because they realize that they will never have the popular support to do so. Instead they vote for people like Barack Obama and the Liberal members of the Supreme Court – people who at first swear to uphold the Constitution, but then when it comes time to truly uphold it they do the exact opposite. Liberals applaud this utmost form of judicial activism, while Conservatives cannot understand how anyone can morally or legally swear to uphold something and then immediately thereafter do everything in their power to actively subvert it, all in the name of "good intentions". But, according to Daniel Webster, "*Good intentions will always be pleaded for every assumption of authority. It is hardly too strong to say that the Constitution was made to guard the people against the dangers of good intentions. There are men in all ages who mean to govern well, but they mean to govern. They promise to be good masters, but they mean to be masters.*"

If you do not believe that Liberals ignore the Constitution, the following is a quote from Alan Dershowitz, a well-known Liberal civil liberties lawyer and friend of the Clintons, "*We, the People of this country, have no unalienable rights... all our rights are subject to modification... the Constitution of the United States of America is nothing more than a piece of paper and... our government should not be restrained by the Constitution because our government can do good things for people.*" Or, as dangerously stated by former President Bill Clinton, "*If the personal freedoms guaranteed by the Constitution inhibit the government's ability to govern the people, we should look to limit those guarantees.*"

6 THE FOUNDING AND MEANING OF THE REPUBLIC

The American experiment of establishing a government by the people was truly unique historically, because it is the only known endeavor in all of modern human history where the common people got together and debated and designed their own form of government. In contrast to their oppressed past, these people simply wanted to live in peace and to be free. They wanted the freedom to go where they wanted, to read what they wished, to worship as they desired, to work their own land, to be able to associate freely and to raise their children into a better life than the tyranny they had been subjugated to in England. To put into perspective what the American experiment meant to our country's founders, and what it should mean to every one of us, Alexander Hamilton wrote to all Americans on October 27, 1787 in the Federalist papers #1 the following amazing and sobering words:

> *"After an unequivocal experience in the inefficacy of the subsisting federal government, you are called upon to deliberate on a new Constitution for the United States of America. The subject speaks its own importance; comprehending in its consequences nothing less than the existence of the UNION, the safety and welfare of the parts of which it is composed, the fate of an empire in many respects the most interesting in the world. It has been frequently remarked that it seems to have been reserved to the people of this country, by their conduct and example, to decide the important question, whether societies of men are really capable or not of establishing good government from reflection and choice, or whether they are forever destined to depend for their political constitutions on accident and force. If there be any truth in the remark, the crisis at which we are arrived may with propriety be regarded as the era in which that decision is to be made; and a wrong election of the part we shall act may, in this view, deserve to be considered as the general misfortune of mankind.*

The Federalist Papers were in response to the Constitution of September 1787, which at that time had been referred to by many as a "bundle of promises", but to many others was something far more ominous – the creation of a centralized federal government – a government that would rule the country autocratically over the sovereignty of the states, similar to the oppressive English aristocracy from which the people had only recently escaped. As a result, the Federalist Papers were written as essays by "Publius" to the American people to allay their reservations and to educate them about the newly proposed government. These papers were so well written that they successfully won the public's confidence and vote, and as a result the

Constitution was ratified and the new federal government was created against the wishes of the anti-Federalists. It is important to note that both sides - the Federalists, who were for a very limited federal government, and the Anti-Federalists, who were opposed to any federal government at all - were against forming any federal government that would have nearly unlimited powers, of the type we have today.

Few people understand that our founding fathers looked at the strengths and weaknesses of all previous governments before they chose the best pieces from which to create their new form of a representative Republic. These investigations are chronicled in the Federalist Papers 15-22. With regards to their choice of a representative republic over a true democracy, Madison in Federalist 10 wrote.

> "*From this view of the subject it may be concluded that a pure democracy, by which I mean a society consisting of a small number of citizens, who assemble and administer the government in person, can admit of no cure for the mischiefs of faction. A common passion or interest will, in almost every case, be felt by a majority of the whole; a communication and concert results from the form of government itself; and there is nothing to check the inducements to sacrifice the weaker party or an obnoxious individual. Hence it is that such democracies have ever been spectacles of turbulence and contention; have ever been found incompatible with personal security or the rights of property; and have in general been as short in their lives as they have been violent in their deaths. Theoretic politicians, who have patronized this species of government, have erroneously supposed that by reducing mankind to a perfect equality in their political rights, they would at the same time be perfectly equalized and assimilated in their possessions, their opinions, and their passions.*

In spite of these great historic words, and in direct contradiction to the principles upon which America was founded, from time to time Liberal professors, who really do not like this country and who are looking for ways to rationalize their distaste of it, publish comparisons that triumphantly (for them) show that America is for example "19th" on the hierarchical list of countries that adhere to true democratic principles. But, these people forget that America is not a true democracy, nor would it last long if it were. America is a representative Republic founded on democratic principles.

John Adams stated, "*There is no good government but what is republican. That the only valuable part of the British constitution is so; for the true idea of a republic is "an empire of laws, and not of men." That, as a republic is the best of governments, so that particular arrangement of the powers of society, or in other words, that form of government which is best contrived to secure an impartial and exact execution of the law, is the best of republics.*" That the American form of government is indeed Republican in nature, the following is written in Article IV, Section 4 of the Constitution, "*The United States shall guarantee to every State in this Union a Republican Form of Government, and shall protect each of them against Invasion; and on Application of the Legislature, or of the Executive (when the Legislature cannot be convened) against domestic Violence.*"

7 THE FIRST AMENDMENT – FREEDOM OF (NOT FROM) RELIGION

We American Conservatives strongly believe in the freedom of religion, where every man has the right to his own religious beliefs, as long as they are not injurious to others, and that religious persecution is not only just as bad as racial or class discrimination, it is the precursor to secularism, totalitarianism and servitude, whether enforced by government or by other groups of men. The reason that religious principles are important to society is that they provide the fundamental morality on which all societies must be based to survive. For totalitarian governments to come to power and to succeed they must first suppress or outlaw the religious beliefs of the people, because those beliefs represent a faith in something more important and more fundamental than the government being forced on them by men, and as such they stand as a bulwark against oppression.

The First Amendment of the Constitution states, "*Congress shall make no law respecting an establishment of religion, or prohibiting the free exercise thereof...*" Importantly, this is the only reference to religion in the entire Constitution. But, a basic tenant of the Liberal platform is that codified somewhere in the Constitution, either hidden in context or somehow intended in meaning, there is a clause that orders a "separation of church and state". However, no such clause exists, nor was it ever intended to exist by the founders, at least not as presently defined by the Left. And, very importantly, the founders did not separate God from state.

What the Left is attempting to do in the US, and it is succeeding, is to expunge the Christian religion from the public square and to secularize America. This is a threat to this country that cannot be understated. While I myself am not religious, I do not fear religion, and I truly believe that society without some form of religion cannot exist. And, as the Left increasingly secularizes America with outright insanity like you can't say Merry Christmas, you must say Happy Holidays, even though holiday means Holy Day, we see our society slowly falling apart.

The Left's dislike of religion is profound. But Conservatives understand that a belief in something greater than man and government is not only inherent to our founding principles it is essential to our society. School shootings, higher rates of poverty due to single motherhood and the greedy religion of the Left, where other people owe "me", are all symptoms of a society in which morality is disappearing in favor of the me, myself and I entitlement way of thinking, as espoused by Obama and the Liberals. School shootings did not occur in the 1950', 1960's, etc., even though it is a statistical fact the more people owned guns in America percentage wise then than they do today. When most of us older folks were kids, we knew what was right and what was wrong from our religious teachings and we feared that God would punish us for something we did, even if no one else was around to ever know. That kind of force for right and deterrence against wrong is absent in a godless society.

As a Conservative, I and others have been attacked for being part of the Republican Party, because the Party has in part a religious base. We have been lectured by Liberals who state "religion has no place in politics" and "all of you Republicans are just a bunch of religious nut cases". First and foremost, many of the Conservatives I know are not personally religious, as I am not. Secondly, politics and government is of the people, by the people and for the people and, as such, people who are religious have the same right to representation of their views in the public arena as does anyone else. Yet Liberals want to take that right away from religious people in this country, but they want to do so primarily from those who are Christian. So, what are Liberals afraid of? A religious person cannot create new laws that will harm you - only government can do that. Religious people cannot force you to believe what they believe - only government can do that. Religious people cannot imprison you or take your possessions at the point of a gun - only government can do that. The Liberal fear and hatred of Christian people is not only misguided, it is dangerous. Yet, Liberals love big government, with all its power to control your life and imprison you by force if you do not comply.

The Liberal hatred of Christianity includes removing the Bible from our courts, so we can no longer swear, "*To tell the truth, the whole truth and nothing but the truth so help me God.*" These days we can no longer display the 10 Commandments, or a Nativity scene, or a cross in any public place. People cannot get together and quietly pray on federal public property, such as in front of the Vietnam War memorial, and our children cannot say the pledge of allegiance at school. As well, pictures of Christian entities, such as God, are prohibited from being displayed. And all of this is while the federal government (Obama) can somehow force priests to hand out condoms to children at mass.

So, why do Liberals so vehemently hate the Christian religion? After all, statistics show that at least 65% of all Democrats are religious in some form or another. This dichotomy is because, first and foremost, amongst all other issues Liberals worship at the altar of abortion. As a result, many of them hate the Christian religion, because it is the world's primary moral force against abortion. Yet, oddly enough, Liberals are strongly supportive of Muslims, while these people are vehemently against all tenants of modern society and want to return to the Dark Ages of theocratic rule. In fact, if anything, the Muslim religion is the purest example of what most Liberals would classify as an ultra-far *right* wing philosophy. And, by the way, Muslims do not believe in abortion either. Also, Liberals do not want anyone to believe that there is something more important, or of a higher moral authority, than their dearly beloved government.

Importantly also, Liberals dislike the Christian religion because it teaches morality in the context of what is right and what is wrong. Liberals on the other hand do not believe in morality. Rather they view any moral teachings as equated with, and as an imposition of, religious views, which they see as offensive, even though religion is not a prerequisite of morality. They believe that it is the government that should control us, and thus a belief in something other than government, such as in morality and (or) in religion, is "dangerous" or "extreme". It is as if Liberals are misbehaving little children, disliking their parents because they were reminded that certain behaviors are morally unacceptable and that certain disciplines will result. Thus they ignore the message of what is right and wrong and demonize all of the messengers who understand these differences.

In a recent article, Jay Alan Sekulow, Chief Counsel of the American Center for Law and Justice, warned, "*Individuals of all faiths or none, and from all points on the political and ideological spectrum, should be alarmed at the mounting assault on the free exercise of religion and freedom of religious expression. The erosion of one constitutional right—especially one as fundamental as religious liberty and the freedom of speech—may serve as a precedent for the erosion of other rights to the detriment of all Americans*".

I will predict that next in the line of Liberal persecution and intolerance towards Christians will be laws that ban people from wearing crosses on necklaces at work (this is already being considered in Great Britain), that ban crosses from being displayed in public cemeteries and (or) that remove "In God We Trust" from being displayed on our American currency. And, even practicing the Christian religion may well be considered illegal at some point, with those who break the law become either subject to prosecution or perhaps to outright termination, as was done in recent history in Germany and Russia and is being done today throughout the Middle East. After all, intolerance is, in and of itself, the opposite of tolerance, leaving no room for compromise or understanding, especially when it comes to the fundamentalist Liberal hatred of the Christian religion and of Christian Americans.

Frighteningly to many, but either ignored or celebrated by most Liberals, in June 2007, (then) Presidential candidate Barack Obama declared that the USA was no longer a Christian nation and in 2010 Obama canceled the 21st annual National Day of Prayer ceremony at the White House under the ruse of "not wanting to offend anyone." Yet on September 25, 2009, from 4 am until 7pm, a National Day of Prayer for the Muslim religion was held on Capitol Hill beside the White House, with over 50,000 Muslims attending. Does anyone not see these actions by Obama and of the Left as both worrisome and telling of their religious cognitive dissonance?

Could the current lack of morality in this country be made up by institutions other than religious ones? Yes, it could, but along with religion the Left has been adamant about expunging all moral teachings from the public arena, so unless the children get such teachings from their parents, whom not enough do, we will soon have more and more generations of children that will grow up in America without a clear moral compass. The one-sided secularization of America has already led to a decline of the country's moral and social structure and this decline will continue, if left to the Liberal mindset.

8 THE FIRST AMENDMENT – FREEDOM OF SPEECH, PRESS AND ASSEMBLY

While Conservatives strongly believe in free speech, as codified in the First Amendment of the Constitution, "*Congress shall make no law .... abridging the freedom of speech, or of the press; or the right of the people peaceably to assemble, and to petition the Government for a redress of grievances*", Liberals appear to only believe that the speech they support is "free". Thus, they want to ban Conservative talk radio by invoking the "Fairness Doctrine", which is anything but fair, and they have an entire lingo of speech that to them is politically correct, while no other language usage is somehow allowed. The political correctness of the Left is an outright infringement on, and attempted censorship of, the free speech of others. The Left's "politically correct" speech is not the speech of Conservatives or others, it represents their politics, and as such the Liberal desire to squelch the free speech of others is akin to soviet-style censorship.

Inherent in the free speech portion of the First Amendment is protection for freedom of the press. This is because our founders understood that, for liberty to survive, the press must be kept free from government censorship and control. As a result of these founding principles, the press in the US for years has been referred to as the Third Estate. However, in the last 30 years or so, a majority of the mainstream press in America has been taken over by Liberals to such a great extent that these institutions voluntarily act like state-owned enterprises, supporting all Liberal ideals and demonizing Conservative concepts in the most vile ways, excluding of course the only objective TV station on the air, Fox News, which is demonically hated by the Left. The self-anointed unqualified support of the Left and the outright censorship of the Right by the mainstream alphabet channel press is a real threat to this country and is in complete opposition to the reason freedom was given to the press in America by our founding fathers to begin with – to ensure the survival of liberty and freedom in the country through maintaining the freedoms of expression and opposition in the public square.

With regards to outright Liberal opposition to the rights of Conservatives, not only with regards to free speech but also to assemble and to petition the Government for a redress of grievances, while the Left champions and applauds any manner of foul speech and outright lawlessness by Liberal groups such as the Occupy and Union labor movements, they publicly ridicule, regale and deride the primarily older folks that are part of the Tea Party Movement. Without a doubt, the American Tea Party Movement is one of the purest examples of a peaceable petition to the Government for a redress of grievances in modern time. But again, this unfortunate but true example of the hypocrisy of Liberals, of trying to silence older people in America just because they think differently than they do, is a clear example of Leftist ideology, where you are for free speech as long as your group has that right, but you would happily deny the same freedom of speech to others, if you could, because they think differently than you do.

The attempt to silence the free speech of the Tea Party and of Conservative groups and individuals by government became even more real recently, and chillingly so, with the disclosure that the IRS since 2009 has been targeting Conservative groups for audits, harassment and the rejection of tax exempt statuses. This is an undeniable and an incontrovertible case of an abuse of power and of government tyranny at work. Now it appears that similar targeting by the EPA has occurred. This targeting amounts to outright voter suppression, to suppressing the political views of those that disagree with Liberal policies and to the absolute infringement of our nation's First Amendment rights. For our democratic system of government to work, political speech must be kept free, otherwise opposing views can be ignored, or worse silenced, by dictatorial gulag-like government methods, thereby allowing America to turn into a dictatorship, as is already dangerously happening under the Obama administration.

So, what are some of the other methods used by Liberals in this country try to stifle the free speech of others? They include using vile appellations at will such as, "racist", "stupid", "Jim Crow", "Nazis", or any other particularly vile name they can think of. But worse yet is their usage of the English language in forming their contempt. The following is a list of recent Liberal incivilities from the website humanevents.com.

1. Teamsters President Jimmy Hoffa unleashed this tirade on Labor Day in Detroit as he rallied the union audience before President Obama addressed the crowd: *"President Obama, this is your army. We are ready to march. Everybody here's got to vote. Let's take these sons of bitches out."*

2. Rep. Andre Carson (D.-Ind.) suggested that some conservative congressmen want to return to the days of lynching. At a Congressional Black Caucus event Miami in August, Carson delivered this gem of civility: *"This is the effort that we are seeing of Jim Crow. Some of these folks in Congress right now would love to see us as second-class citizens. Some of them in Congress right now*

with this Tea Party movement would love to see you and me ... hanging on a tree."

3. Vice President Joe Biden used an AFL-CIO rally in Cincinnati on Labor Day to mock the political opposition in vile terms. Biden told the union members: *"You are the only folks keeping barbarians from the gates."*

4. House Minority Leader Nancy Pelosi, at a San Francisco fund-raiser, said Republicans were sacrificing their children in their attempt to destroy government: *"The Republicans right now are using the idea of deficit reduction as an excuse, they're hijacking an idea that has some resonance—we all want to reduce the deficit—in order to not reduce the deficit but to destroy the public space, destroy government. ... You wonder, do their children breathe air? Do they drink water?"*

5. California Rep. Maxine Waters (D.-South Central) revved up her constituents in a recent meeting by blasting the Tea Party and talking tough. Waters told the crowd: *"I am not afraid of anybody. This is a tough game. You can't be intimidated. You can't be frightened. And as far as I'm concerned, the Tea Party can go straight to hell."*

6. Al Gore, high priest of the global-warming cult, likened those who question his doctrine to racists: *"There came a time when friends or people you work with ... when racist comments would come up in the conversation and in years past they were just natural. Then there came a time when people would say, 'Hey, man, why do you talk that way? I mean that is wrong. I don't go for that, so don't talk that way around me. I just don't believe that.' That happened in millions of conversations and slowly the conversation was won. We have to win the conversation on climate."*

7. Political genius and hack comedienne Janeane Garofalo came up with a doozy of a conspiracy theory, positing that the Koch brothers or Karl Rove or Grover Norquist were paying Herman Cain to run for President in order to deflect charges of racism against Republicans. Taking off her tinfoil hat to appear on Al Gore's Current TV, Garofalo said: *"Herman Cain, I feel like, is being paid by somebody to be involved and to run for President so that you go, 'Oh, they can't be racist' ... There may be a touch of Stockholm syndrome, because anytime I see a person of color or a female in the Republican Party or the conservative movement or the Tea Party, I wonder how they could be trying to curry favor with the oppressors."*

8. Keith Olbermann, the former MSNBC host now working for Al Gore's Current TV, was infuriated by the debt-ceiling deal and called on his viewers to share his anger (luckily for America he has few viewers): Those

responsible for the debt-ceiling deal, Olbermann said, *"will crush us, because those who created it are organized and unified and hell-bent. And the only response is to be organized and unified and hell-bent in return." Opponents of the deal "must find again the energy and the purpose of the 1960s and early 1970s, and we must protest this deal and all the goddamn deals to come, in the streets."*

9. After his call for civility following the shooting of Arizona Rep. Gabrielle Giffords, President Obama's failure to condemn Hoffa's remark gives tacit approval for more shameful attacks. After sharing the same podium with Hoffa at the Labor Day rally where the labor leader declared war, the President has refused to condemn the remarks, with a presidential spokesman saying the President isn't going to *"serve as the speech police of the Democratic Party."*

10. As Democratic bile worsens, abated by President Obama's blinders, it was only time before the culture became infected with violent anti-conservative imagery. The video-game company StarvingEyes has released a new game called "Tea Party Zombies Must Die," *where impressionable young minds can score points by killing zombies in the likeness of Sarah Palin, Michele Bachmann, Newt Gingrich and Fox News hosts.*

As disgusting as these examples of Liberal behaviors are, by Obama and other Liberals mostly since Obama was elected, I believe that we have not yet seen the worst, and I cite numerous further examples of the cognitive dissonance of Liberal behaviors in the following sections.

9 THE SECOND AMENDMENT – THE RIGHT TO KEEP AND BEAR ARMS

The Second Amendment of the Constitution states, "*A well regulated Militia, being necessary to the security of a free State, the right of the people to keep and bear Arms, shall not be infringed*". Conservatives in America strongly believe in the right to bear arms, because as our founding fathers were so aware of, governments can be corrupted by unrestrained power and the most important way to start the process of enslaving a population is to take away their guns, so that they cannot defend themselves against advancing tyranny.

As stated by George Washington, "*A free people ought not only to be armed and disciplined, but they should have sufficient arms and ammunition to maintain a status of independence from any who might attempt to abuse them, which would include their own government.*" Also, as written by Thomas Jefferson, "*The strongest reason for people to retain the right to keep and bear arms is, as a last resort, to protect themselves against tyranny in government.*"

How much more ridiculous an argument can there be in this country than the one being made by the Left even now that when every time there is a violent gun episode we should ban the tool rather than to deal with the cause? As if banning anything, such as drugs or illegal immigration, or anything else for that matter has been effective at all in this country. Also, the Liberal response against different kinds of firearms, or clip sizes, or calibers, is, "Why do you need that for hunting?" But in fact the Second Amendment and the right to bear arms has nothing whatsoever to do with hunting and nothing to do with need. It is about the populace having a right of last resort to protect themselves against threats, whether they are external or internal, against other individuals or against the force of government.

Because the Second Amendment is so simple and so clear, the Left's primary argument against the Amendment, combined with their hatred of it because they are virulently anti-gun, is that the phrase "*well regulated Militia*" means something other than what is stated. For the record, in the late 1700's, well regulated was used to mean well-appointed or properly equipped. And a militia was that portion of the civilian populace that was willing to bear arms in support of the country, as further explained in the historic quotes below.

George Mason stated, "*I ask sir, what is the militia? It is the whole body of the people except for a few public officials. To disarm the people is the best and most effectual way to enslave them...*" Tench Coxe further clarified, "*The militia, who are in fact the effective part of the people at large, will render many troops quite unnecessary. They will form a powerful check upon the regular troops, and will generally be sufficient to over-awe them*". Further, the following statement was published in the Pennsylvania Gazette, on February 20, 1788, "*Who are the militia? Are they not ourselves? It is feared, then, that we shall turn our arms each man against his own bosom. Congress have no power to disarm the militia. Their swords, and every other terrible implement of the soldier, are the birthright of an American... The unlimited power of the sword is not in the hands of either the federal or state governments, but, where I trust in God it will ever remain, in the hands of the people.*"

So, while we have clear historical clarification of what constitutes a militia, as well as why the founding fathers believed so strongly in the right to keep and bear arms, you will still hear Liberals today making contorted ridiculous arguments against the Second Amendment, obfuscating that a militia only means the police, and therefore the populace has no right to bear arms, or that the founding fathers only foresaw that right for hunting purposes only. These are utterly ridiculous arguments, but you will hear them stated over and over by Liberals, because these arguments are their only defense against what is otherwise brilliantly clear and simple language by our country's founders.

With regards to recent attempts to outlaw certain types of rifles, particularly "assault rifles" in a January 3, 2013 article, AWR Hawkins wrote that, "*According to the FBI annual crime statistics, the number of murders committed annually with hammers and clubs far outnumbers the number of murders committed with a rifle… In 2005, the number of murders committed with a rifle was 445, while the number of murders committed with hammers and clubs was 605. In 2006, the number of murders committed with a rifle was 438, while the number of murders committed with hammers and clubs was 618. And so the list goes, with the actual numbers changing somewhat from year to year, yet the fact that more people are killed with blunt objects each year remains constant. For example, in 2011, there were 323 murders committed with a rifle but 496 murders committed with hammers and clubs… Another interesting fact: According to the FBI, nearly twice as many people are killed by hands and fists each year than are killed by murderers who use rifles.*" It is important to note that these statistics cover rifles of all types and that the number of people actually killed each year with "assault rifles" is actually only a very small subset of the total numbers presented. Yet Liberals would have you believe that thousands are killed every year in the US, by "assault weapons", which by definition are not actually truly assault weapons at all, unless they have a three selection function

1) semi-automatic fire, 2) three round burst, and 3) fully automatic fire, which they do not.

Obama, who has lied to the American people for four years stating that he supports the Second Amendment, is now pushing for new draconian gun laws, as a result of recent gun violence. With regards to Obama's "new" anti-gun position, let's first remember what Obama said in 2008, which was, ""*I just want to be absolutely clear. Alright, so I don't want any misunderstanding when you all go home and you are talking to your buddies and you say, ah 'He wants to take your guns away.' You've heard it here, I'm on television so everybody knows it. I believe in the Second Amendment. I believe in people's lawful right to bear arms. I will not take your shotgun away. I will not take your rifle away. I won't take your handgun away.*"

But, in direct contradiction to what he said in 2008, Obama recently used the executive branch to try to outlaw certain guns in America, by way of 23 executive orders, as his way to circumvent congress (something he should be impeached for). This is in spite of the fact that there are an estimated 20,000 gun laws already on the books in the US. And, while Obama wants more laws, including more background checks, the laws that are in place are not being upheld. For example, data from the National Criminal Justice Reference Service (NCJRS) found in 2010 that"*...of 6 million Americans who applied to buy a gun, less than 2 percent -- or 76,000 -- were denied. Of those, the ATF referred 4,732 cases for prosecution. Of them, just 44 were prosecuted, and only 13 were punished for lying or buying a gun illegally.*" Also, a study done by Syracuse University found that "*...the number of federal weapons prosecutions fell from about 11,000 in 2004 to about 6,000 under the Obama administration in 2011.*" This was in spite of a doubling in gun sales.

With regards to the Fast & Furious scandal, in which weapons were illegally sold at the government's request to obvious Mexican cartel straw buyers and then were used to kill Mexicans and a US Border Patrol agent, many believe that Obama instituted this program silently so as to use those gun sales to Mexico as an underhanded way to institute new gun laws. Any rational person has to question this program, because in fact the government never tracked the guns after they were sold.

Regarding the efficacy of stricter gun laws, in a recent article (March 28, 2013) by the US News it was revealed that, "*The districts that contain Chicago, Los Angeles and New York City ranked last in terms of federal gun law enforcement in 2012, according to a new report from Syracuse University's Transactional Records Access*

Clearinghouse, which tracks federal data… These cities also have some of the nation's most restrictive gun laws, as well as the most active mayors in championing gun control. New York Mayor Michael Bloomberg, Chicago Mayor Rahm Emanuel and Los Angeles Mayor Antonio Villaraigosa are all members of the national Mayors Against Illegal Guns campaign." These cities also have some of the highest firearm related murder rates.

The foregoing are clear examples of how Liberals and Obama first and foremost willfully do not adhere to the nation's gun laws and secondly how they will do anything they can to circumvent the American system of limited powers by the federal government, including the unconstitutional use of executive "powers" to strip Americans of their constitutional right to keep and bear arms. And they continue down this path in spite of laws on the books that they do not even prosecute. This is because they simply do not want Americans to have the option of last resort against government tyranny, and that is an armed rebellion. Why? Because they want to use the federal government to control the people – that is their agenda, that is what they believe in and that is what they are doing in America today – and they want no opposition whatsoever.

But most chillingly yet, Obama announced recently that he will sign a U.N. arms treaty, in a clear attempt to bypass our nation's gun laws and the Constitution by using a foreign agreement to implement a backdoor gun registration policy in America. This shows how Obama has clear contempt for American jurisprudence and sovereignty and how he does not care one whit about the Constitution or about the American way of life or our history.

It is very instructive to note that, while America has the world's highest per capita gun ownership, having an estimated 92 gun owners per 100,000 residents, it has a relatively low overall homicide rate compared to other countries, totaling only 4.7 homicides per 100,000 population And, this number has dropped by half since 1992, as gun ownership has gone up.

Talk about stupidity in government. The constant saber rattling about gun control by Liberals during Obama's first four years in office has resulted in the unprecedented sale of more than 70 million firearms in the US, an increase of greater than 100% more firearms purchased under Obama than were acquired during George W. Bush's first term in office. So, Liberals, you might actually want to blame yourselves and Obama for the 35+ million extra guns that are in the hands of Americans as a result of your anti-gun policies…

This is while the Department of Homeland Security, a domestic organization, is now being investigated for planning to purchase 1.4 **billion** rounds of hollow point ammunition to use against its own citizens, ammunition that is banned worldwide for use in human warfare.

10 OTHER FEDERAL "RIGHTS"

We Conservatives do not believe that inherent in the Constitution there are federal "rights" to such things as abortions, healthcare, condoms, cell phones or to any other form of federal government largess in which money is taken from one individual or group of individuals strictly for the personal gain of another or for groups of others. This perceived right by Liberals, of the federal government to take wealth from one group simply to redistribute it for the benevolence of another group, is simply not in the Constitution of the United States and is not legal at the federal level. There are precisely 17 federal powers that are enumerated in Article 1 Section 8 of the Constitution (see Constitution included herein at the end) - all other powers are reserved to the states.

The abuse of federal power by Obama and the Left is nothing short of appalling. This is especially true with regards to their support of endless welfare commitments, in order to bribe people to vote for them - commitments that are not only unsustainable, they are unconstitutional. It is an absolute fact that the Constitution grants no power to the federal government to redistribute the nation's wealth to others. James Madison explained that "*the government of the United States is a definite government, confined to specified objects. It is not like the state governments, whose powers are more general. Charity is no part of the legislative duty of the government.*" Also as stated by James Madison, "*I cannot undertake to lay my finger on that article of the Constitution which granted a right to Congress of expending, on the objects of benevolence, the money of their constituents.*" Or, as stated by President Franklin Pierce in his 1854 veto of a measure to help the mentally ill, "*I cannot find any authority in the Constitution for public charity. [To approve the measure] would be contrary to the letter and spirit of the Constitution and subversive to the whole theory upon which the Union of these States is founded.*"

That is not to say that function of societal largess should not be, or cannot be, fulfilled by the states or by private groups, such as by charities and the churches, because as stated by the 10th Amendment, "*The powers not delegated to the United States by the Constitution, nor prohibited by it to the States, are reserved to the States respectively, or to the people.*"

11 STATES' RIGHTS

While Conservatives are derided constantly by Liberals because we are alleged by them as being selfish and uncaring of our fellow man, Conservatives actually believe strongly in helping people, but we believe that such assistance is best given at the state level or by private charities, not by the detached, supremely inefficient and out-of-touch federal government. And, constitutionally, that kind of help is reserved to the states, should the states wish to do so, because, again, "*The powers not delegated to the United States by the Constitution, nor prohibited by it to the States, are reserved to the States respectively, or to the people.*" Conservatives believe that government assistance is most effective at the state and community level, because the people that live in the community are the ones who know best about the circumstances and situations of the recipients.

Conservatives also believe that it is a state's right to decide whether or not to allow abortions in that state. However, Liberals are well aware that the majority of people in many if not most of the states will not vote for Liberal ideals like abortion. So, to get their Liberal agenda approved, and to force that agenda on the unwilling states and on local populations, they intentionally use the federal system to get their way. How many votes are there by the people at the state level that have been overturned recently by some Liberal federal judge appointed by the likes of Obama or by other Liberals before him? In these cases, the Left uses judicial fiat to do what they cannot do locally - and that is to win at the ballot box. This is why Liberals do not really believe in state rights at all, but rather prefer to use the federal legal system, and if possible the Supreme Court, to force their views on others by way of federal judicial tyranny. And that is why Liberals support people like Obama for president – because Obama is a person who abhors states' rights and is willing to ignore those rights, acting essentially the same as any third world country's dictator.

So what are "states' rights" and why are they preserved in the Constitution? According to our American form of government, except for the 17 enumerated powers of the federal government, all rights are reserved to the states. This was done by our founding fathers so that there could be a federal government, with its protections for the people, while at the same time limiting the power of government so that the states could remain truly sovereign. After all, it was the states - not the federal government - that gave us our liberties.

In a 2011 Blog by Bruce Walker entitled "Preserving States' Rights and the Constitution" he writes, "*Federal power is fractured into a bicameral legislature, a presidency, and a federal court system. The powers of the federal government are spelled out in plain language, and the Tenth Amendment declares that powers not given to the federal government in the Constitution are kept by the states. The first amendment adopted after the Bill of Rights, the Eleventh Amendment, was specifically to limit the power of federal courts over state governments.*

Why were Americans so concerned with states' rights? States made the American Republic a marketplace of governments. If states are preeminent in the governance of the nation, then when one state slides towards tyranny, people can leave and move to another state. When groups want to find a place to live in peace, like the Mormons in Utah or Jews in New York, strong states ensure that they can do so.

It is a grim fact of history that strong central governments have gone hand in hand with horror. Nazis, very quickly, essentially ended the system of strong state governments in Germany. The Soviet Union was also ruled with an iron hand from Moscow, and the destruction of whole peoples followed its central policies. The closer people are to the elected officials governing them, the more freedom flourishes. The more remote the government, the less citizens feel like equals and the more they seem like cattle. That is why the Founding Fathers considered states' rights as absolutely indispensable to the purposes of our nation."

In direct contrast to the structure of our American government as set forth by our nation's the founders, and in a complete refutation of the all of the warnings of history regarding large centralized governments, Obama and Liberals love the federal government and abuse it at the expense of states' rights. These abuses by Obama, including using the government to spy on American citizens, who have done no wrong, and using the IRS and EPA to squelch the free speech of others is now at a dangerous level never before seen in America. And in this regard remember the words of Benjamin Franklin, "*They that can give up essential liberty to obtain a little temporary safety deserve neither safety nor liberty.*" These abuses by the Left have risen to the undeniable level of government tyranny and are in direct contradiction to our nation's laws and to our founding principles. But, this is what happens when you vote for someone who has no respect for America, as we Conservatives warned repeatedly to no avail in 2007 and 2008 and again in 2012.

12 PERSONAL PROPERTY RIGHTS

The foundations of the Declaration of Independence, the Constitution and to our nation's laws and ethics, that of universal equal rights, were laid much earlier in history by Augustine, Thomas Aquinas, Robert Bellarmine, Hugo Grotius and by John Locke, a 17th century English philosopher. Locke was the first to argue that "*persons own themselves and their labor, and that when a person works that labor enters into an object and that object then becomes the property of the person*". As well, as stated by fee.org, "*Locke established that private property is absolutely essential for liberty: every Man has a Property in his own Person. This no Body has any Right to but himself. The Labour of his Body, and the Work of his Hands, we may say, are properly his. The great and chief end therefore, of Mens uniting into Commonwealths, and putting themselves under Government, is the Preservation of their Property.*"

Locke believed further that the human rights to Life, Liberty and Property are inalienable. His concepts were expanded on by our country's founders into the timeless statement, "*We hold these truths to be self-evident, that all men are created equal, that they are endowed by their Creator with certain unalienable rights, that among these are life, liberty and the pursuit of happiness.*" Accordingly, the relationship between property rights and our other freedoms was extensively protected by the country's founders in the Constitution, including in Amendment 5, "...*nor shall any person ... be deprived of life, liberty, or property, without due process of law; nor shall private property be taken for public use, without just compensation.*" Also, in Amendment 14, "*No State shall make or enforce any law which shall abridge the privileges or immunities of citizens of the United States; nor shall any State deprive any person of life, liberty, or property, without due process of law; nor deny to any person within its jurisdiction the equal protection of the laws.*"

So, what is the definition of property? The definition includes "something owned or possessed" and "something to which a person or business has legal title to". Therefore, a person's property is their land including their home, their financial assets, their other material holdings and even their labor. Consequently, by extension, to take a person's property is to take the fruits of their labor and is enslavement, and to take their labor is to also take their property, which is enslavement as well, whether it is in part or in whole. As stated in the Virginia Bill of Rights, "*That all men are by nature equally free and independent, and have certain rights, of which, when they enter into a state of society, they cannot by any compact deprive or divest their posterity; namely, the enjoyment of life and liberty, with the means of acquiring and possessing property, and pursuing and obtaining happiness and safety.*" Also, as stated by John Adams, "*The moment the idea is admitted into society that property is not as sacred as the law of God, and that there is not a force of law and public justice to protect it, anarchy and tyranny commence.*"

However, in direct contradiction to the nation's founding, and almost in direct agreement with the main tenants of Communism, Liberals do not believe at all in personal property rights. And they especially will not admit the real fact that the taking of property from an individual or a group without their permission can be equated with government sponsored slavery and even to a stand against the most fundamental of all rights - the right to life.

Examples of Liberal's disdain for personal property rights include environmentalism, where either the federal or state government can throw you in jail for things you do on our own land, including now especially using the EPA or the Army Corp of Engineers to take your personal property rights from you. Examples of this include a father and son in Florida who were thrown into federal jail for several years because they filled in a depression that had water in it in their own back yard (that case and their freedom was eventually won by the Pacific Legal Foundation). And the Liberal disdain for property rights also includes the impacts of taxation. For example, many elderly people have lost their homes in California and in other states because they could not pay for huge increases in property taxes that resulted from value appreciation – something that is inherently wrong. But worse yet, Liberals believe in and practice asset forfeiture. In "Civil Forfeiture Laws And The Continued Assault On Private Property", Chip Mellor writes, "*Civil forfeiture laws represent one of the most serious assaults on private property rights in the nation today. Under civil forfeiture, police and prosecutors can seize your car or other property, sell it and use the proceeds to fund agency budgets -- all without so much as charging you with a crime. Unlike criminal forfeiture, where property is taken after its owner has been found guilty in a court of law, with civil forfeiture, owners need not be charged with a crime let alone be convicted to lose homes, cars, cash or other property.*"

As well, Liberals strongly believe in confiscating the wealth of some – the "rich" - for the benevolence of others, as part of their socialist redistributive ideology. The Liberal disdain of personal property rights even extends to unjust incarceration, for example where as many as 64 people have been recently slated for release from federal jail for gun ownership "crimes" that they did not commit.

As stated by Daren Jonescu, "*Progressivism, as its most prominent advocate these days tells us, represents the desire to "spread the (that is, your) wealth around" by means of government coercion. Progressivism is the advocacy of so-called positive rights, i.e., claims against other men grounded not in human nature, but rather in a vindictive ideologue's wish list. Progressivism is the balkanization of society based on income strata and their corresponding layers of resentment. It is a fundamental denial of even the possibility of individual achievement, in favor of the antitheory that all goods are ultimately the product of collective, centrally planned action -- that "you didn't build that," that no human being ever ultimately achieved anything, but rather the state achieved everything. Progressivism is, in sum, the rejection of the individual, which means of individual human nature, which means of individual natural rights. Where there is no rights-bearing individual, there is, needless to say, no self-ownership; there is no concept of "my labor" and "my time"; therefore, there is no product of "my efforts." Property does not exist. Allow me to emphasize this point. For progressives, private property is not merely to be "sacrificed" in the name of some higher good. Their goal is much more profound: property is to be refuted.*"

In a separate article, Jonescu writes, "*Government is the provider, the facilitator, the ultimate source of all individual success. Thus, government has a legitimate (and seemingly unlimited) claim on the results of individual success. The upshot of all this for the question of property is undeniable: private property is an illusion, the selfish fantasy of those who ignorantly believe that their possessions are the earned fruit of their labor. Your prosperity is the product not of your effort and skill, but rather of the general social conditions in which it was achieved. The public roads, the public education system, and other government projects which form the common background of practical existence obviate any inviolable claim you might make on anything you have acquired against that background. You owe your wealth to society, because "somebody else" (i.e., government) made it happen.*"

At the same time that Liberals disdain the very property rights that have existed in America for centuries, they try to convince Americans that they really have other property "rights"; ones that have never actually existed, such as a "right" to Social Security, healthcare, welfare, etc. So, while Liberals are most happy when they are forcefully taking the property of others, they scream bloody murder and march in the streets when budget cuts impact what they perceive as their "right" to various forms of property from the government, but of which no one in their right mind would ever actually consider to be a "right" at all.

But perhaps even worse yet, Liberals frequently argue that, due largely to socioeconomic status, the rightful property of another belongs to someone else, when in fact it does not. Examples include draconian rent laws, particularly in California where, when someone rents your home, they have more legal right to it, your own property, than you do. Another example is the Liberal rhetoric since 2008 about the "banks taking homes away from the people". But the fact is, when you purchase a home but have not yet paid for it, that home is not yours – it belongs to the deed holders. You don't actually own that home until you pay for it in full and receive the deed in your name. These fundamentally immoral approaches are prime examples of Liberal cognitive dissonance. In other words, not only did you "not build that" you don't even really own it, according to Liberal ideology.

The Liberal assault on private property rights is one of the most dangerous ideologies that this nation faces. Think about it. If your personal property rights are taken away, Liberals can do almost anything to you, including taking your home, your guns, your wealth and even your children. If, for example, you have no private property, including yourself, then you have no right to self-defense, or to stand your ground against an oppressor, and your guilt or innocence is subject to the court of Liberal personnel opinion, where you are guilty of "murder" if the attacker is a minority, or in some way disadvantaged, or a Democrat, no matter the circumstances of the attack, as was exemplified recently by the George Zimmerman case where he was deemed guilty by Liberals just because of the race of the victim. If we lose our personal property rights, then justice is lost, it has no meaning whatsoever and anarchy reigns.

Most folks do not realize this, but while they think that they have a right to "privacy", what in fact is privacy? It can be argued that there can be no privacy without private property - that you can only really be private within the confines of your home, or the private homes of others, or in your motor home, car, etc. Therefore, the Liberal onslaught against property, including private property, is really an attack on privacy. Locke's inalienable rights to life, liberty and property by extension argue that a free people cannot have any one of those rights without having the other two, and that there is no right to privacy without all three.

In the Preamble to a Congressional Resolution, Benjamin Franklin wrote, "*Whereas, whenever kings, instead of protecting the lives and property of their subjects, as is their bounden duty, do endeavor to perpetrate the destruction of either, they thereby cease to be kings, become tyrants, and dissolve all ties of allegiance between themselves and their people...*" Remember also the timeless words of Abraham Lincoln, "*Property is the fruit of labor...property is desirable...is a positive good in the world. That some should be rich shows that others may become rich, and hence is just encouragement to industry and enterprise. Let not him who is houseless pull down the house of another; but let him labor diligently and build one for himself, thus by example assuring that his own shall be safe from violence when built*".

Once America goes down the path of ignoring the fundamental association between the ownership of property and liberty, and between a person's labor, their property and their privacy, anything can be justified, including the taking of life, liberty and property at the behest of the "state", such as was done by Hitler and other totalitarian governments to millions historically and is being done by Obama and the Left more and more today.

13 THE CONCEPT OF CLASS IN AMERICA

The Liberals, and especially Obama, are obsessed with class warfare. Not only do they fabricate different classes of people and single out different groups and interests for either special attention or debasement, they intentionally pit American against American in an effort to gain power and support. Conservatives do not believe in this. We believe that no one is entitled to anything other than to life, liberty and the pursuit (not the guarantee) of happiness in our great nation. As such, we believe that all men are created equal and should be afforded equal access. But, more importantly, we also believe that with rights come responsibilities.

Irrespective of the Liberal class warfare, do classes of people really exist in America? This depends on your definition, whereby any population can be split into different categories or classes. But, Conservatives generally argue that America is classless, in that all of our nation's laws apply to each and every one of us, not just to certain groups. Also, we are all Americans and it has been noted by the IRS that in any 10 year period approximately 65% of the people in any of the various income classes are no longer in that "class" after 10 years, having moved up or down in income level.

The concept of class is used by the Left and by Obama as an emotional bludgeon, as their prime example of what they believe is wrong with America and as a divisive tool to foster their own power and support. If you take Obama's constant reference to the "middle class" and replace it with the word "proletariat", and replace the term "millionaires and billionaires" with the word "bourgeoisie", you will see that he is in fact arguing the same class warfare as did the communists in recent history. As well, you will notice that Obama and the Left actually repeat and support the famous words of the communist Karl Marx, "*From each according to his abilities, to each according to his needs.*" For those of you who think that President Franklin Delano Roosevelt's New Deal was something other than the main start of socialism in America at the federal level, please compare the words of Marx quoted above to FDR's own words, "*Here is my principle: Taxes shall be levied according to ability to pay. That is the only American principle.*"

For those who may not have read them, and to see how closely the main tenants of communism are mirrored by the beliefs of the Left, it is illustrative to include the ten planks of the Communist Manifesto below, although #8 could be called decidedly Conservative with regards to the work obligation when compared to the modern Liberal way of thinking:

1. *Abolition of property in land and application of all rents of land to public purposes.*
2. *A heavy progressive or graduated income tax.*
3. *Abolition of all rights of inheritance.*
4. *Confiscation of the property of all emigrants and rebels.*
5. *Centralization of credit in the banks of the state, by means of a national bank with state capital and an exclusive monopoly.*
6. *Centralization of the means of communication and transport in the hands of the state.*
7. *Extension of factories and instruments of production owned by the state; the bringing into cultivation of waste lands, and the improvement of the soil generally in accordance with a common plan.*
8. *Equal obligation of all to work. Establishment of Industrial armies, especially for agriculture.*
9. *Combination of agriculture with manufacturing industries; gradual abolition of the distinction between town and country by a more equable distribution of the population over the country.*
10. *Free education for all children in government schools. Abolition of children's factory labor in its present form. Combination of education with industrial production.*

14 "RIGHTS" VS. RESPONSIBILITIES

Do you ever notice that when a Liberal talks about his or her "right" to healthcare or to whatever right they believe they are entitled to, that he or she actually means that someone else should be forced to pay for that "right", using the federal government to collect the money from others at the point of a gun or by incarceration if need be? As well, have you noticed how numerous these Liberal "rights" have become recently, including the "right" to same-sex marriage, a "right" to an abortion, a "right" to free contraception, a "right" to free Internet access and cell phones, the "right" to force everyone into a Union and a "right" to a certain wage and benefits, to name a few? And, in particular have you noticed how willing Liberals are to march loudly in defense of their "rights" and to create anarchy, believing that only their self-chosen groups of people have these inherent rights? But, all the while, it is clear that Liberals are not concerned with the collateral impacts that these highly selective rights have on the rights of others, whether those other people be in the majority or in the minority.

Liberals never want to talk about their own responsibilities or duties and, in fact, never concede to the concept that with rights come responsibilities, because that would mean they would have to take personal responsibility for their own actions and as well be more mindful of the rights of others. For example, while Liberals espouse their various rights, you will notice that they never respond to questions about those rights by saying, "I think my family has a right to [insert any Liberal "right" here] so I and I alone have the responsibility to provide it". The fact is that they cannot admit to a connection between rights and personal responsibilities, because the Liberal welfare state can only survive by the unequal portioning of those rights, with the fruit of the rights being the provenance of the takers while the responsibility of paying for those rights becomes the obligation of the makers, all rationalized by using such twisted concepts as "fairness", "social justice", "economic justice" or "equality".

In direct contradiction to the Liberal mindset, we Conservatives believe that a right is something that does not impinge on another person's rights, and that the rights that we do have in society are limited to life, liberty, the pursuit of happiness, and the equal rights guaranteed to every citizen under the nation's laws. Importantly, Conservatives also believe that individual rights cannot be taken away by another person or by groups of people, including government, nor can rights be conferred to certain individuals, or to certain groups, in preference to or above others. In other words, Conservatives believe that everyone in America, and in fact every human being in the world, has the same inalienable rights. But, we also believe in responsibilities, including a personal obligation to protect not only your rights but also being mindful of the rights of others, so that liberty is preserved not just for the individual, but for all of society. The following quotes provide some historical perspective to these Conservative principles.

With regards to the belief that individuals rights cannot either be conferred or taken away by others, such as those in government, Ayn Rand wrote, "*Individual rights are not subject to a public vote; a majority has no right to vote away the rights of a minority; the political function of rights is precisely to protect minorities from oppression by majorities (and the smallest minority on earth is the individual)*". And, with respect to the relationship between an individual's rights and the rights of others, Thomas Jefferson wrote that, "*Rightful liberty is unobstructed action according to our will within limits drawn around us by the equal rights of others. I do not add 'within the limits of the law' because law is often but the tyrant's will, and always so when it violates the rights of the individual*".

About rights and responsibilities, or duties, Pope John XXIII wrote, "*In human society one man's natural right gives rise to a corresponding duty in other men; the duty, that is, of recognizing and respecting that right. Every basic human right draws its authoritative force from the natural law, which confers it and attaches to it its respective duty. Hence, to claim one's rights and ignore one's duties, or only half fulfill them, is like building a house with one hand and tearing it down with the other*". And, finally, with regards to responsibilities, Eleanor Roosevelt wrote, "*Freedom makes a huge requirement of every human being. With freedom comes responsibility. For the person who is unwilling to grow up, the person who does not want to carry his own weight, this is a frightful prospect*".

In spite of the quoted wisdom of many great people, what Liberals are constantly championing and doing today is the exact opposite of these ideals, because they believe in empowering the many to take from the few, in allowing the rights of the minority to be taken away by a tyranny of the majority and in promoting the twisted concept where only certain classes of people have rights, whereas for others there is only the responsibility to pay for those "rights". Examples include Obama's persecution of the "rich", or the upper 2% of wage earners, through unequal taxation and the Liberal concept of economic class rights, where the "poor" somehow have the right to free services but have no responsibility to pay for them. The constant talk about Liberal rights by Obama resonates with the Liberal masses, because they actually believe that government money exists, and that it is endless, such that all they have to do is to tax the "rich" to receive any right they can greedily dream of, without having to take responsibility for anything, much less for themselves. But in the Conservative perspective, the moral reality of this kind of socialistic thinking is so far removed from what is actually just or even fair under our guiding principles it is abhorrent, even without considering the economic situation of the nation. As Margret Thatcher once said, "*The problem with socialism is that you eventually run out of other people's money*". Actually, the real problem with socialism is that it is flawed in every aspect of morality, good judgment and outcome.

15 ABORTION

Conservatives strongly believe that our children are our national wealth, our heritage and the future of this great nation. And we believe that to wantonly and shamelessly kill them in the womb is true mass genocide.

As an example of the greatest genocidal event in all of human history, since the passage of Roe vs. Wade, over 55 million children have been killed in America through the godless ideology of the Left - abortion. These numbers are comparable to the mass slaughters perpetrated by Moa Ze-Dong (~50 million), Hitler (~21 million) and Stalin (~20 million). In order to rationalize their twisted ideology, Liberals use the most ridiculous arguments for abortion, and then defend them with anger because even they know that the arguments they make are not really rational at all.

The Liberals first argument for abortion is that somehow abortion is a women's "right to choose", which is yet another example of Liberal rights. However, many states have laws against women harming their babies through, for example, drug use where the child can be taken from the mother permanently after delivery. So, the woman somehow has a right to choose to kill her child, but she does not have a legal right to otherwise harm the child in the womb. Just as illogical, in some states a person can be charged with a double homicide if that person's actions result in the death of a woman and her unborn fetus - yet the women has a right to kill that same child and somehow that is not considered a homicide. Also, Liberals argue that a child is not really a human being with any rights at all, until he or she is born. Yet from the moment that child is conceived, it is a scientific fact that it is simply a maturing human being that is yet to be born. As well, in one of the greatest dichotomies of all time, Liberals are against the death penalty because it is "cruel and unusual punishment", yet they are for killing a child in the womb, extending even to Obama's voting twice against a law in Illinois that would have protected children born alive outside of the womb from being killed by the doctor after a botched late-term abortion (the law was eventually passed in spite of Obama's twice-over opposition).

While US population growth has fallen below the sustainable level, without having immigration, many in the Liberal community argue that the 55 million children killed should have been aborted because they "could not be taken care of". But this argument is nonsense and does not take into account the real statistics of why children are aborted in America - especially when other countries that are poorer have significantly higher population growth rates, and thus children, and they take care of them fine. The stated reasons for women having an abortion from the National Right to Life website are: "*Feels unready for child/responsibility - 25%; Feels she can't afford baby - 23%; Has all the children she wants/Other family responsibilities - 19%; Relationship problem/Single motherhood -8%; Feels she isn't mature enough - 7%; Interference with education/career plans - 4%; Parents/Partner wants abortion - 1%; Other reasons - 6.5%*". So, we are killing generations of children, because in some cases the woman "feels unready for child/responsibility", or "has all the children she needs", or "feels she isn't mature enough" or worse yet "it interferes with her plans".

Liberals also forget the terrible lifelong toll that abortion takes on many women. An analysis of the impact abortions have on women was recently published in the prestigious British Journal of Psychiatry. "*The report was the most extensive of its kind to date -- the author looked at 22 published studies and data from more than 870,000 women. The results showed that women who have an abortion are at an 81 percent increased risk for mental health problems, including anxiety disorders, depression, drug abuse and suicidal behaviors. The study revealed the shocking statistic that close to 10 percent of all mental health problems in women can be directly attributed to abortion*".

The real problem with the current abortion law in America is that it is a federal law and to be such a majority of the Supreme Court had to find somewhere in the Constitution that there is a constitutional right to an abortion. However, I defy any rational person to find that right anywhere in the Constitution. And, because that right simply does not exist, the decision for Roe vs. Wade has to be considered one of the most glaring examples of Liberal-minded judicial activism in the history of this country. Again, this is an example where the "pro-choice" Liberals had to use the federal system for their judicial fiat, because they knew that most of the states would not vote for pro-abortion laws.

The true ending story for the Roe vs. Wade lawsuit is the rather sad circumstances of Norma McCorvey, who was "Roe" in the federal pro-abortion lawsuit. This woman was used by the left, because the Liberal female plaintiff's lawyers, "*…were looking for a woman who wanted an abortion, but did not have the means to obtain one. An adoption attorney introduced them to Norma McCorvey. They needed a plaintiff who would remain pregnant without traveling to another state or country where abortion was legal, because they feared that if their plaintiff obtained* *an abortion outside of Texas, her case could be rendered moot and dropped".* So, these Liberal lawyers used a woman who in fact falsely claimed she was raped to have an abortion to be part of a federal lawsuit that they knew would take years to resolve. Accordingly, the decision did not come in time for Norma McCorvey to have the abortion she sought, so instead she gave birth to her child, whom she later put up for adoption. McCorvey is now vehemently anti-abortion and believes that she was misled and was shamelessly used by the Left to get what they wanted – US wide abortions.

It should be noted that according to Wiki Answers, "*The baby's heart beat can be seen on an ultrasound at around 7 weeks, and if you are very slim MAY be heard on a Doppler from 9 or 10 weeks. You can start to hear the babies heartbeat through ultrasound as soon as 6 weeks into your pregnancy!*" That means that likely before someone knows for sure that they are pregnant their babies heart is already developed and beating – yet Liberals will tell you that the baby is not yet a human, nor is it alive and it certainly is not yet worthy of protection.

The illustrate the appalling sickness of the abortion loving Left, in a recent (March 29, 2013) article in the Weekly Standard, "*Florida legislators considering a bill to require abortionists to provide medical care to an infant who survives an abortion were shocked during a committee hearing this week when a Planned Parenthood official endorsed a right to post-birth abortion. Alisa LaPolt Snow, the lobbyist representing the Florida Alliance of Planned Parenthood Affiliates, testified that her organization believes the decision to kill an infant who survives a failed abortion should be left up to the woman seeking an abortion and her abortion doctor. "So, um, it is just really hard for me to even ask you this question because I'm almost in disbelief," said Rep. Jim Boyd. "If a baby is born on a table as a result of a botched abortion, what would Planned Parenthood want to have happen to that child that is struggling for life? "We believe that any decision that's made should be left up to the woman, her family, and the physician," said Planned Parenthood lobbyist Snow.*

So, similar to what Obama argued for twice, we should now be able to even kill children outside the womb. So, should we all consider the "doctor" who does that for a living as a compassionate, caring healthcare professional (Liberal definition) or a sociopathic murderer of defenseless babies (Conservative definition)? Truly, what human being could actually perform in particular late term abortions, and what kind of society could sanction such horrific deeds? Well, read the next paragraph to hear about just such a person and how horrific these deeds really are.

CNS News reported on April 19, 2013 that, "*On the last day of testimony before the prosecution rests in the murder trial of abortionist Kermit Gosnell, a former worker at Gosnell's clinic testified that she saw one late-term baby who survived an abortion "swimming" in a toilet and "trying to get out." Kareema Cross, a "medical assistant" who worked at Gosnell's Women's Medical Society clinic for four-and-a-half years, testified in a Philadelphia court today, telling of the horrors of babies who survived abortions only to have their necks snipped with scissors. "Did you ever see those babies move?" asked Prosecutor Joanne Pescatore. "Yes, once in the toilet," said Cross. The baby "was like swimming," she said. "Basically, trying to get out." Adrienne Moton, an employee at the clinic, then took the baby and snipped the back of its neck while its mother was still in the room. Cross told the jury that when Shayquana Abrams came into the clinic in July 2008 she was pregnant, "and she was big." When the baby was born alive, Abrams was sleeping. Cross said Dr. Gosnell took the baby boy, which she described as 12 to 18 inches long, and put him inside a plastic container the size of a shoebox. "The baby was still breathing," she said. "He didn't cut the neck right there." The baby was too big for the plastic container, with his arms and legs hanging over the sides. "The Doctor cut the back of the baby's neck but didn't do suction—normally Dr. Gosnell would do suction … to suck the brains out," Cross said."*

These absolutely horrific deeds by "doctors" in the US, which should make every thinking human being weep, are not reported by the Left and by the Leftist mainstream media, so as to not challenge their appalling support for abortion and in particular for late term abortion. It should be noted that Gosnell did get convicted of three counts of murder, but how many thousands of children per year are legally murdered by these practices, even excluding other abortions?

With regards to the racial aspect of abortions in the US, *Jonathon* Moseley writes, "*It is a fact that Planned Parenthood has killed unborn Black babies by the tens of millions. It is a fact that Planned Parenthood has been far more lethal to Blacks than the KKK. Although African-Americans make up 12% of the U.S. population, they account for nearly 35% of all abortions performed. Blacks accounted for nearly 423,500 of the 1.21 million abortions performed in 2008.*" In spite of this, Planned Parenthood is the Holy Grail of Liberals and of the Democrat Party - to the tune of around $540 M per year.

The Declaration of Independence starts with these powerful words, "*We hold these truths to be self-evident, that all men are* ***created equal,*** *that they are endowed by their Creator with certain unalienable Rights,* ***that among these are Life****, Liberty* *and the pursuit of Happiness".* My friend John Dreier points out that, "*For some years I have noted that life, liberty and the pursuit of happiness mentioned in the Declaration of Independence are hierarchical values - to be free you must be alive and to pursue happiness you must be free. Thus life is higher up the ladder than freedom and freedom is higher up than is the pursuit of happiness. The pro-abortionists turn this truth on its head by making a woman's pursuit of happiness more important that the unborn person's life. Biologically, there is no doubt that life begins at conception. Genetically, at that moment a new person is created.*"

Who then in America is willing to fight for our Constitutional rights for the soon to be born, or for the just recently born, especially for their Right to Life? Is it the Conservative or the Liberal? We all know the answer to that question.

16 CHARITY

Studies after study have shown that Conservatives/Republicans give more to charities than do Liberals by large margins. But, does that mean they are all richer? A Liberal would tell you so, but that simply is not true. For example, Vice President Joe Biden's tax records show for years he earned plus $200,000 in annual salary but gave only a total of $3,690 over a ten year period to charities, or about a dollar a day. The same holds true for Barack Obama, who is a multi-millionaire. With regards to studies that highlight the differences in giving, as reported by the New York Times, "*Arthur Brooks, the author of a book on donors to charity, "Who Really Cares," cites data that households headed by Conservatives give 30 percent more to charity than households headed by liberals. A study by Google found an even greater disproportion: average annual contributions reported by Conservatives were almost double those of liberals.*

Obama has campaigned on the platform of taking away the charitable tax deduction for private charity, and he plans to do so. He has stated clearly and repeatedly that charity is the function of the federal government, and he has in fact proposed legislation to essentially wipe out philanthropy in America by getting rid of the tax deduction for charitable giving. Conservatives are outraged at this, because churches and other important charitable institutions cannot exist in this country without private charity. Yet Obama wants to destroy this very important pillar of American life, in favor of gaining more government control over people's lives.

I will remind the Liberal populace that the government is the least effective way to administer charity. Government largess is not only supremely inefficient, with people rarely receiving what they really need, but it comes at a steep price – a huge inefficiency and a waste of most of those precious resources. And perhaps most importantly, government aid is not true charity at all - it is the government compelling people by force through taxation under the threat of incarceration to give up their property for the "good" of others.

True charity is when a man or a woman gives freely to another or to a cause, doing so of their own free will, because they truthfully want to help other people. Obama's stated desire to federalize charity is an outrage that every American should oppose, no matter your political philosophy.

17 DIVERSITY

Liberals worship at several shrines, but included amongst these is the shrine of "diversity". According to them, diversity, which is defined as ethnic diversity or multiculturalism, is good for society - it is a goal to be achieved in all areas, from equal numbers of different groups in education, to neighborhoods and even to the extent of forcing diversity in areas where it is perceived to be lacking. But, what is a healthy functioning society? To have a healthy society, you must have a population that has the same cultural identity and the ability to understand one another philosophically, to work together and to communicate within a common region. This means that a healthy society must have a common language, border and culture. But cultural diversity, which goes hand in hand with ethnic diversity, has been found to have a negative, not a positive, impact on society.

Michael Jonas, in an article called "The Downside of Diversity," published in Boston.com in 2007, encapsulated research by Harvard political scientist Robert Putnam in his 2000 book on declining civic engagement, in which Jonas states that Putnam, "*-- has found that the greater the diversity in a community, the fewer people vote and the less they volunteer, the less they give to charity and work on community projects. In the most diverse communities, neighbors trust one another about half as much as they do in the most homogenous settings. The study, the largest ever on civic engagement in America, found that virtually all measures of civic health are lower in more diverse settings*".

What other negative impacts are there to society as a result of the Liberal "diversity" movement? Jay Haug points out that college campuses are less tolerant than they were before because, "*One result is that real debate and dialog suffer. The Atlantic's Wendy Kaminer explains why. 'One of the ironies of this drive for civility ... [is that] you end up encouraging incivility, because people don't know how to argue. They don't know what to do when confronted with an idea they really don't like. They don't have an administrator they go complain to, and so they* just *shout it down because they haven't learned how to do anything else'*." He also points out that, "*People who hold traditional views on marriage and other issues are wrongly dismissed as bigoted, homophobic, or in need of being cured, Embracing diversity in household formation blinds us to the reality that children of lasting man-woman marriages fare best, The diversity movement confuses rejection of views with rejection of people, shutting off debate, and Diversity as it is proclaimed is fundamentally dishonest*". He states that, "*The diversity movement is not only deeply flawed; it is also far from a harmless ethos with no consequences for our culture, our values, or our institutions. It is time to acknowledge that diversity often results in the opposite of what it so loudly proclaims: a closed-off world that stifles debate, learning, and mutual respect.*" Selwyn Duke points out that, "*If one blindly accepts the unproven assertion, "Our strength lies in our diversity," one may join Clinton, Chris Matthews, and other languid-minded leftists in a leg-tingling love-fest. But the reality is that diversity isn't a strength to be applauded -- it's an obstacle to be overcome. To understand this, you only have to study history and consider the fate of the former Yugoslavia: the Balkans are balkanized because of diversity. And now the United States is being balkanized, too.*"

In fact it is worthwhile to note that the 1960's, Martin Luther King and others on the Left correctly espoused the benefits of integration, with the societal goals most famously described by MLK in his "I Have a Dream" speech as, "*I have a dream that my four little children will one day live in a nation where they will not be judged by the color of their skin but by the content of their character.*" But now, in diametric opposition to those famous words, Liberals champion the concepts of multiculturalism and diversity over integration, although they will try to convince you that these are all compatible ideals, when in fact they are not. These concepts are not the same, because the term "integration" assumes the development of common bonds and beliefs, or as defined by The Free Dictionary as, "*The bringing of people of different racial or ethnic groups into unrestricted and equal association, as in society or an organization; desegregation.*". However, the term "diversity" is rooted in the concept of disparity, which is defined as, "*utterly different or distinct in kind; unlike things or people; from Latin disparāre to divide.*" Similarly the societal definition of multiculturalism is, "*the policy of maintaining a diversity of ethnic cultures within a community.*"

While Liberals would and do force on communities and groups their ideas of diversity, they ignore the facts that cultural diversity is not necessarily good for society, and indeed they do not even understand that diversity is the opposite of integration and thus that they have strayed very far indeed from MLK's dream of true cultural integration for America. This is not to say we as a country do not want immigrants, nor do we want to be completely homogenous, but in order to have a healthy society we must have the same language, border and culture and thus be integrated as a society. This should be self-evident to everyone, but to the Left's alter of diversity worship, the exact opposite is true, and the negative effects on America society as a result of these Liberal ideologies are becoming more and more evident every day.

18 EDUCATION

Providing a proper education to our children and to our young people is the most important function we can provide as a society today, because a well-educated populace is essential to the future of our country and for the well-being of our citizens, especially in an increasingly technology oriented society. But, what has happened to education in America over the last 40 years, a period in which the federal government has spent $1.8 trillion on education, and spending per pupil in the United States has tripled in real terms?

The numbers below are real statistics that highlight the Liberal vs. Conservative divide regarding education in America – a divide that perhaps in no other arena is more consequential to the nation's future and one that highlights perhaps best the differences between the two philosophies - Liberals believing that more and more spending on education will solve all of our problems, whereas Conservatives point out that massively increased spending on education in recent years has not resulted in improved outcomes.

Recent studies have shown that America ranks #2 worldwide on spending per student for education, just slightly behind Norway. However, in spite of this massive spending level, in which "*Government at all levels spent an average of $149,000 on the 13-year education of a high school senior who graduated in 2009*", another 2009 study found that '*U.S. students ranked 25th among 34 countries in math and science, behind nations like China, Singapore, South Korea, Hong Kong and Finland.*" Studies also show that foreign students are outranking their American peers on an accelerated basis. For example, "*Just 6 percent of U.S. students performed at the advanced level on an international exam administered in 56 countries in 2006. That proportion is lower than those achieved by students in 30 other countries.*" And, a more recent study, which provided a better breakdown of US education performance and a noteworthy comparison, concluded that "*Students in Shanghai who recently took international exams for the first time outscored every other school system in the world. In the same test, American students ranked 25th in math, 17th in science and 14th in reading*". Please note that the statistics quoted above are from the Huffington Post, an ultra-Liberal blog.

With regards to basic skill levels and national graduation rates in the United States, the Heritage Foundation reports that, "*National test scores reveal that many students are failing to master basic skills. On the National Assessment of Educational Progress, 33 percent of fourth-graders score below basic in reading, as do 26 percent of eighth-graders. According to the Department of Education, fourth-graders not performing at a basic level are unable to make general conclusions about what they read. At the eighth-grade level, this means students are unable to make simple inferences or interpret ideas. For both grade levels, these are crucial skills to master to ensure future academic success. In addition, a poor grasp of basic content knowledge means children are exiting high school unprepared for college or the workforce, if they even graduate at all. National graduation rates have stagnated around 73 percent, with numbers significantly lower for minority students. In 2006, only 61 percent of Hispanic students and 59 percent of Black students graduated. An independent analysis found that, in some of our nation's biggest cities, fewer than half of all students finish high school. In the Baltimore City and Cleveland Municipal City school districts, only about one-third of all students graduate. Indianapolis has a graduation rate of only 30 percent, and a mere 24.9 percent of Detroit students complete high school. These shockingly low graduation rates should incite a national outrage. And while some politicians will surely call for investing more tax dollars for public school as the solution, a lack of funding is not the source of the problem".*

So, why is America so poor at educating and graduating its children? The problems are multi-faceted but Conservatives believe that the fault lies first and foremost at the feet of the Federal Department of Education, a bloated federal bureaucracy that Conservatives want to get rid of, but that Liberals adore. Conservatives ask, "What does this bureaucracy actually do for education in the US?" We Conservatives believe that the answer is, "It spends vast sums of money but without positive results". Proof of this comes from many studies. For example, according to Lindsay Burke of the Heritage Foundation, "*In August 2012, the White House released the report 'Investing in Our Future: Returning Teachers to the Classroom" to bolster President Obama's call for massive new education spending. The report suggests that, absent an enormous infusion of more tax dollars, the nation's public schools will lose teachers and programs, damaging American education. This claim ignores the fact that over the past 40 years, both teaching and non-teaching positions in public schools have increased at far greater rates than student enrollment. And, of all education jobs, teachers make up only half… From 1970 to 2010, student enrollment increased by a modest 7.8 percent, while the number of public-school teachers increased by 60 percent. During that same time period, non-teaching staff positions increased by 138 percent, and total staffing grew by 84 percent. Not surprisingly, the more than doubling of non-teaching staff since 1970 has meant that teachers are a smaller proportion of school payrolls. Since 1970, the percentage of teachers as a portion of school staff has declined by 16.5 percent. Teachers now comprise just half of all public-school employees.* However, as also stated by Burke, "*More teachers are teaching fewer students, as the student–teacher ratio has continued to decline. According to the NCES, the student–teacher ratio for fall 2012 will be slightly greater than 15:1.*"

So, the reality is that America spends almost the highest amount per capita on education of any country, but has some of the poorest results and an overall declining trend in competitive educational quality, due at least in part to an emphasis on bureaucracy over teachers, even though student-to-teacher ratios are at some of the lowest levels they have been in the last 40 years. The latter statistic is in direct contradiction to Liberals repeatedly contending that student-to-teacher ratios have increased dramatically in the US in recent years and that a declining number of teachers is the primary reason for poor comparative education outcomes, such that even more government spending is needed.

Conservatives believe that education in the US is substandard due to a number of reasons, but an important component of poor quality is due to Liberal influences. These influences include teaching at "the lowest common denominator", where children are discouraged from excelling in some classrooms, because excellence may cause the poorer students to have lower "self-esteem", according to some Liberals. As a result, the education our children are receiving in many areas has been dumbed down, including not even grading children at certain levels, instead of accelerating our best and brightest over the poorer students, such as is done in the British education system. But, most importantly, less and less of the basic skills, such as reading, writing, arithmetic and consequential history, are taught in favor of teaching environmentalism, Liberal social ideologies and very selective revisionist Liberal history. It is shocking to find out that cursive writing is no longer taught in the US after the 3rd grade and that most of today's high school graduates cannot read cursive.

With regards to Liberal social ideologies, in a recent article in American Thinker by Daren Jonescu, Jonescu states, "*I examined the particular evils of current public education systems, modeled as they invariably are on some version of post-Marxist, Dewey-inspired progressivism, according to which the primary function of education is to strip young citizens of their virtue, individualism, and self-reliance, and to replace these prerequisites of a free, civil society with nihilism (an emptiness that the state can fill with its neo-religious agendas), collectivism (which breeds hatred of those who do not accept the state's agendas), and class envy (which provides the state with a perpetual scapegoat for all its inevitable failures to create the prosperity it promises)...*" Further he states that, '*Every day, parents are sending their children to a place where they will be taught: (a) that getting along with others is the primary social skill, regardless of who the "others" are and what they are doing; (b) that failing to follow the latest trends in music (lust, hate, violence), fashion (slovenliness, sexiness, disrespectfulness), or social behavior (drugs, drinking, sexual pressure) will make you a "loser" among your peers, and -- at best -- a pity case among the teachers; and (c) that excelling is only appreciated or encouraged within the range of achievement set by the curriculum (agenda-driven drivel), class average (lower every year), and teacher expectations (finish the textbook on time)... A visitor from only fifty years ago would be shocked to learn that in today's North American schools, Shakespeare, Austen, Donne, and Swift are out; lifestyle choices, green studies, and diversity are in."*

Another real problem with our education system, and one that cannot be solved no matter how much federal money is spent, is the highly documented correlation between single motherhood and poor academic achievement. According to Trevor Thomas of American Thinker, "*Children from single-parent homes are twice as likely to be suspended or expelled from school and are more than twice as likely to be arrested for a juvenile crime. According to the U.S. Department of Health and Human Services, 85% of children with behavioral disorders don't have a father at home. Children living without dad are much more likely to abuse drugs, commit suicide, and run away from home. They are more likely to have lower academic achievement along with lower self-esteem. Children born to unwed mothers are about seven times more likely to live in poverty than children with fathers in the home. The correlation between fatherless homes and the negative effects on the family is irrefutable.*"

So, should we continue to increase funding, as demanded by Liberals and by Obama, to fix our nation's educational problems? The answer is, historically, that decades of increased funding for public education have not led to better outcomes. A new Heritage Foundation report found that, "*... education spending is at an all-time high, and student performance has flat lined. The report details a 23 percent real increase in per-pupil spending in the past decade and a real increase of 49 percent over the past 20 years. With these figures in mind, it is hard to make the argument that a lack of funding is the problem. Per-pupil spending has more than doubled since 1970, yet academic achievement has remained flat*".

The statistics quoted above show how a bloated federal bureaucracy, run by Liberal politicians and Left-leaning teachers, actually can and does have a negative impact on education in the US, in part by increasing bureaucracy and inefficiency, but also through negative influences due to Liberal teaching methods, in spite of massive funding increases. As well, we have a US wide teachers union, with archaic nonsensical rules such as you cannot fire underperforming teachers. In spite of these facts, Liberals cannot conceive of returning something as important as education from a federally mismanaged system to a more efficient system run at the state level by people in the community who, in close cooperation with the parents, know what is best for our children. In fact, Liberals have now succeeded in getting a standardized curriculum called Common Core accepted in 36 states. This curriculum consists of far left wing ideologies and removes education once step further from our local community to being run by the federal government, primarily as a Liberal indoctrination camp.

A sad fact that few are aware of in America is that only about 2,000 of our total 130,000 public and private schools are responsible for a high percentage of the nation's total dropouts. In these schools, which are considered "majority minority" schools, test scores are at failing levels and have not improved for 15 years, dropout rates average 40% or higher and the children that do graduate mostly cannot read or write. Sadly, it is Liberal policy to ignore these failings, because these sub-substandard results lead us to a different conclusion than Liberals would have us believe - that the entire system of K1-12 education in America is flawed. Worse yet, as our educational system fails generation after generation of especially Black children, the problem is ignored by Obama, a Black man, who really does not care at all about the plight of Black children in this country. But, perhaps we should be fairer to Obama and admit that his hands may be tied somewhat. After all, if you are beholden to the teachers union, which he is – a union that does not want to change anything - then you can't really support the children at the expense of your union membership support. How disgusting is that?

In contrast with huge increases in K1-12 funding, college education across America has been receiving less and less funding from state governments for years. This problem is exacerbated most in the far western states, which are run almost exclusively by Democrats. For example, whereas the University of Washington was funded almost 100% by state contributions some 25 years ago, now only a paltry 16% of University expenditures are funded by the state, making the old designation of "state funded higher education" a joke. So, while some vote for Democrats because they believe they are pro-education, the opposite is actually true, and the states in which college-level university funding has been cut the least actually are those that are under Republican governor and (or) legislative control.

So if more money alone isn't the answer to K1-12 education, and it clearly has not been, what will lead to better academic improvements? We Conservatives believe that the entire public school system, which is built on Leftists agendas, enforced mediocrity and inferior standards, needs to be reformed by, 1) limiting federal involvement and returning education to the community level, 2) allowing choice in home schooling and private schools, 3) creating standards for education and teachers supported by testing and appropriate hiring/termination practices, 4) increasing more parental involvement and control through parent education by having parent input into teacher/administration and hiring/firing practices, and 5) promoting a strengthening of the family structure. Accordingly, all federal spending on education should be re-reviewed under the harsh reality of poor current outcomes, where exorbitant spending has proven ineffective in combating high dropout rates and outright illiteracy.

Our children are our future and it is our responsibility to them and to our society to give them the educational tools they need to survive and to prosper, or America will continue to decline, especially in the future standard of living and wellbeing of our children and grandchildren.

19 ENERGY INDEPENDENCE

Harry Reed and Barrack Obama have been quoted numerous times saying "*With only 2% of the world's oil reserves, we can't just drill our way to lower gas prices. Not when we consume 20% of the world's oil.*" This is an obfuscation used by the Left to promote their anti-oil, environmental extremism agenda. The facts, as reported by government agencies such as the United States Geological Survey and others, are far different. For example, as reported by Calvin Beisner of Master Research "*The U.S. has 22.3 billion barrels of proved reserves; a little less than 2% of the entire world's proved reserves, according to the Energy Information Administration. But as the EIA explains, proved reserves "are a small subset of recoverable resources," because they only count oil that companies are currently drilling for in existing fields.*

So, how much recoverable oil does the U.S. really have? From the same source Beisner states, "*Start with the Green River Formation in Wyoming: 1.4 trillion barrels—sixty-two times as much as Obama counts. After Green River, it's almost embarrassing to count other sources: 86 billion on the outer continental shelf; 24 billion in the lower 48; 2 billion on Alaska's North Slope; 19 billion in Utah tar sands; 12 billion in ANWR. Then add in oil shale: 800 billion just in Wyoming and neighboring states. As IBD sums it up, 'When you include oil shale, the U.S. has 1.4 trillion barrels of technically recoverable oil, according to the Institute for Energy Research, enough to meet all U.S. oil needs for about the next 200 years, without any imports'.*"

Also, "*These estimates are almost sure to rise over time—to anywhere from three or four to twenty or twenty-five times as much. Those are the ranges of error on past official estimates of recoverable oil. Here is what Robert Bradley Jr. calculated back in 2000 for the carbon-based energies: Proved oil reserves today are estimated to be fifteen times greater than the original 1948 estimate despite interim production of eleven times this amount. World natural gas reserves in the last thirty years have increased almost five-fold despite interim production that has been 80 percent above the 1967 estimate. World coal reserves today are estimated to be over four times the amount calculated nearly a half-century ago.*

All of these estimates and potential upsides suggest the possibility of another 2.3 trillion barrels of oil equivalent that may yet be discovered in the US. While this number is likely high, new technologies like fracking have proven to be safe and effective ways to increase oil reserves and significant upsides beyond the estimated 1.4 T barrels of recoverable oil are possible.

Just imagine the positive economic impact that becoming energy dependent would have on America and on Americans. The US produces about 4.8 M and imports about 10 M barrels a day. At $115 per barrel oil, the average price of Brent crude for 2012, this equates to $1,150 M per day of our national wealth being exported outside the US, or $419.8 B a year. Being energy independent and possibly being a net energy exporter would substantially bring down the cost of our own oil and greatly boost the economy of the US and all involved in it, which means every American would participate in a better economic future.

But why, instead, does Obama and the left want to waste billions of taxpayer dollars on "green" energy companies, which cannot compete and many of which have declared bankruptcy? Any president who wastes taxpayer dollars such as Obama on outright frauds like Solyndra should be impeached, but instead he is supported by the Left and is heralded by them as a hero of the environmental movement. Why is this? Is it because drilling for oil is so dangerous, yet moving 10 M barrels a day across our world's oceans isn't risky? Nonsense! It has been confirmed that drilling on land and in shallow water is not very dangerous at all, and new drilling techniques have resulted in very safe and clean oil and gas production both on and near shore. However, drilling in very deep waters, as mandated by Obama due to his ban on shallow water drilling, is much more environmentally dangerous, as evidenced by the Gulf BP spill. Yet, Obama supported the more dangerous deep gulf drilling, while prohibiting shallow water development, because it was offshore - out of sight and out of mind.

So, while Obama supports exporting our national wealth oversees, never to return, resulting in fewer high paying jobs and a lower standard of living for Americans, he does so because he garners the support and votes of Liberal environmental radicals. These people are directly responsible for the economic plight of America, yet few Americans recognize this, including almost all Liberals. In fact, Liberals applauded Obama when he repeatedly stated while campaigning for his first term that he wanted to see oil prices rise substantially, to break America of its dependence on oil. Yet we all know, or should know, that this does not work – rather it just creates hardship on Americans. We Conservatives know what Obama and the extreme environmental movement are all about and what these policies are doing to America and to Americans. Do you?

As a geologist and a scientist, it is my responsibility to first look at the real data, before drawing any conclusions about an issue, and then if those conclusions are solid based on the data at hand, I then look at the politics that surround the issue and ask, "Why does either party or both parties support what they do?" Similarly, whether you are a scientist or not, each individual has a responsibility to first look at the data and to read published treatises, both for and against, rather than to mindlessly watch and have their children watch a movie as misguided and factually incorrect as for example Al Gores, "An Inconvenient Truth". But inexplicitly, Liberal parents tend to take what is fed to them by the Liberal government as fact, and instead of questioning why the government supports such a viewpoint and inquiring as to what impact that belief coupled with proposed government policy may have on them and on society, they not only tend to accept such viewpoints blindly, they parrot them endlessly and support them as fact, even for example going so far as to say to scientists who believe otherwise, "*Your belief against anthropogenic-caused global warming is the same as denying that the Holocaust occurred*". Again, this is a prime example of true Liberal cognitive dissonance – a type of insanity without comparison.

Almost every person in the world is concerned about their environment, or should be, and thus we are all in some ways environmentalists at heart. But environmentalism must be tempered with common sense, because if it is not the country will be stymied in its efficiency and production and in its ability to grow and to increase the standard of living of its people, as is occurring now due to the environmental extremist policies being implemented and supported by the Left. So, let us all be clear here, Conservatives as a group are very pro-environment and are for environmental protection, in spite of being portrayed as the "destroyers of land, air and water" by Liberals, who wrongly encourage and foster these misconceptions to promote their own environmental radicalism. And we Conservatives do understand that man can adversely impact the environment and that a certain amount of environmental regulation is not only needed, but that it is desirable. As such, the endless epithets and lies promulgated by the Left against Conservatives and against Republicans, by saying "You Republicans want dirty air, dirty water and to kill our children", including even the President of the United States repeating such insanity, is not only factually incorrect, it is a perversion of self-thinking, self-aggrandizement and outright persecution by the Left against other Americans.

Very briefly, I encourage everyone to look up the Antarctic Vostok ice core climate data that stretches back 420,000 years, to look up the glacial retreat maps for North America and Europe that cover the last 25,000 years and to look at unfiltered climactic temperature data, and the complicated interpretations thereof, before you are so quick to support the "Warmers". Also, read about the climate fraud perpetrated on the world by the IPCC and CRU unit at East Anglia labs. I will not present the data herein. However, I will tell you that I and at least 3,800 of the world's most renowned climate scientists believe that there are no data yet presented that suggest or prove that man has caused the climate to warm during the Industrial Revolution. Importantly, these scientists, as I do, see no correlation whatsoever between CO2 contents and global warming. As well, there is no real evidence of sustained global warming over the last 100 years, and in fact that temperatures over the Holocene Maximum, comprising about the last 10,000 years, have been stable and perhaps are even declining, and temperatures during the last 155 years have remained stable in spite of alarmist models of extreme warming.

So, call me a Global Warming (GW) "Denier", or as some Liberals, such as Keri Norgaard, a teacher at the University of Oregon who compares global warming skepticism to racism, have suggested "*…there is a cultural resistance that keeps some people from acknowledging that humans are responsible for global warming*", and this condition she claims "*... must be recognized and treated as an aberrant sociological behavior*". Or worse yet, perhaps the solution should be invoked as proposed by wacko Richard Parncutt, an Austrian Leftist who teaches at the University of Austria, who stated recently, "*I propose that the death penalty is appropriate for influential GW deniers.*" This insanity is typical of the Left and is eerily reminiscent of the totalitarian rhetoric we have heard in the past from Hitler and others just prior to their state ordered mass executions - either agree with us and be like us, or die…

As a geologist, let me introduce you to an important concept, and that is what is referred to as the "carbonate or limestone cycle". High levels of CO2 in the past, and even now, have led to a greening of the planet, due to plants needing CO2 to survive. In fact, plants prosper at high CO2 levels. For example, even now it is estimated that higher CO2 levels in that last 30 or so years have increased the production of wood from trees by as much as 60 tons per acre. This means that the current high CO2 levels (~380 parts per million), which have been many times higher in the geologic past, have resulted or will result in an explosion of life on the planet. And, as this CO2 becomes dissolved in the oceans, it will also result in an explosion of marine life, much of which uses CO2 plus calcium (Ca) to produce CaCO3, which is calcium carbonate. But the net effect of higher CO2 levels is to stimulate life –life which eventually produces more carbonate rich sediments. These sediments then become lithified and turn into rock (limestone). When this happens, all of the excess CO2 is fixed into rocks, thereby permanently removing it from the atmosphere and from further biological interaction, until such time, if ever, when it may be subducted, partially melted and returned again to the atmosphere in the form of CO2 via gaseous volcanic eruptions. This chemical fact, of the "carbonate cycle", shows how the earth heals itself from high CO2 levels and why high CO2 levels are not to be feared – unlike what Obama and the Liberals want you to believe.

Let's revisit the current CO2 content of the atmosphere mentioned above – 380 *parts per million.* This then equals 0.038% of our atmosphere. And prior to the industrial revolution, CO2 comprised 0.028% of the atmosphere. But the largest quantity "greenhouse gas" is water vapor, which averages 16% of the atmosphere. So, if greenhouse gasses contribute to global warming, why aren't we "regulating" water vapor? Why instead scare people to death with an almost immeasurable increase in CO2 content? Because government wants more of our money and finds it effective to use scare mongering, particularly against an uniformed almost willing populace, to increase taxes based on junk "science".

Many people have forgotten, but in the 1960's and 1970's the US government was warning us of dire circumstances, because they believed that the earth was cooling - not warming. So why use these scare tactics, if indeed the data is not definitive or the science "settled", as suggested by Al Gore and others in an attempt to silence opposition and real science? This is because the government wants to scare the populace into agreeing with the greatest, most destructive series of tax increases ever in the world, so that it will have more of your money and thus more power. And the impact of those policies truly will be destructive.

It has been estimated that the cost of carbon-tax legislation proposed by the Democrats, would at the minimum be a direct cost just for energy to every family in the United States of $2,600 per year. This coupled with higher costs for all manufactured products, farm products and products that must be shipped to markets, which includes everything we use or own, would be significantly higher, with the result that the economy of this country and others would be forced into a deep recession, with perhaps many in the Third World dying of starvation as a result. But these very real consequences are glossed over by Liberals, because they do not examine first the efficacy of the arguments, nor the cost to them and to society, before blindly supporting them out of the very fear that their irresponsible government is trying to force on all of us.

As a precursor to the next four years under Obama, in his January 2013 inauguration speech he said, "*We will respond to the threat of climate change...*" This man is a radical environmental ideologue who pays no attention to science and to fact and even now he is preparing to enact by judicial fiat the next round of carbon tax legislation, with the huge negative impacts that this will have on the world, including the same kinds of impacts that the government mandated ethanol for fuel from food (corn) program had by driving an estimated 70 million people below the sustainable food level into starvation worldwide, due to huge increases in the cost of corn, as reported in 2012 by the WHO (World Health Organization).

This interesting quote from Pravda on January 6, 2013, describes how others in some parts of the world perceive American global warming scare mongering, "*For years, the Elites of the West have cranked up the myth of Man Made Global Warming as a means first and foremost to control the lives and behaviors of their populations. Knowing full well that their produce in China and sell in the West model and its consequent spiral downward in wages and thus standards of living, was unsustainable, the elites moved to use this new "science" to guilt trip and scare monger their populations into smaller and more Conservative forms of living. In other words, they coasted them into the poverty that the greed and treason of those said same elites was already creating in their native lands. What better way to staunch protests at worsening economic and life conditions than to make it feel like an honorable job/duty of the people to save "Gia". At the same time, they used this "science" as a new pagan religion to further push out the Christianity they hate and despise and most of all, fear? Gia worship, the earth "mother", has been pushed in popular culture oozing out of the West for a better part of the past 1.5 decades. This is a religion replete with an army of priests, called Government Grant Scientists.*"

As a scientist and a geologist, I can tell you honestly the greatest fear we should have is that soon we will go into a period of global cooling, followed by another prolonged Ice Age, perhaps lasting as long as 50,000 years. And during that Ice Age, there will be no Canadians and no Europeans, due to the eventual coverage of those northern regions by ice sheets, and it is a fact that mankind in general will have a very difficult time surviving, accompanied by the deaths of perhaps hundreds of millions.

So, be very happy indeed that we are in a period of overall global high temperatures, because I can assure you as a geologist that global cooling is coming at some point, possibly in the very near future and that global cooling will have a catastrophic impact on all of mankind. But, sadly due to the insanity of the Left, some of us may not even survive to the point where the planet starts to cool, having already been exterminated by starvation due to higher taxation and higher food and energy prices - all forced on us as by Liberal absurdity, what Conservatives refer to as environmental extremism, but what Liberals classify as "settled science".

21 FAIRNESS, EQUALITY AND JUSTICE

In the Liberal mindset, it is perfectly acceptable to use the concepts of "fairness", "equality" and "justice" as divisive class weapons to argue their many forms of government promoted inequality and tyranny. From Obama's "*They need to pay their fair share*" to the Liberal concept of fairness being one of equal outcomes versus the Conservative principle of equal opportunity, fairness, equality and justice are the Liberal's primary weapons of choice to use against Conservative ideals. Yet Liberals actually practice the opposite of fairness, equality and justice, because to be fair to one should be fair to all and the concept of equality should be that all men are created equal and therefore the nations' laws should be applied equally to all men and women, regardless of race, religion, or social circumstance. However, the Left argues that this should not be the case, instead promoting decidedly unfair laws in government such as "hate crimes" where the only government decreed "hater" is white, with no prosecution of minorities for hate crimes possible, whether those crimes are committed against other minorities or against whites.

With regards to the many federal programs of socialist government largess promoted by Obama and the Left, the following still holds true, "*And no matter how you slice it, property theft to promote a false ideology of "fairness" or advance a twisted form of "compassion" to gain power is abhorrent.*" It actually is Conservative ideals that champion and promote true fairness and equality, not the Liberal socialist mindset of redistributing the nation's wealth, which is morally and ethically wrong. Cynthia Ward states, "*The claim that wealthy people owe more taxes to government, that it's not fair unless they pay more whenever the country needs it, necessarily embraces certain value judgments that are rarely if ever exposed in political debate. The fairness claim necessarily denies that people have the presumptive moral right to own the money they earn. It necessarily implies that if you do earn a lot of money, that fact alone -- the mere fact that you are wealthy -- makes you a legitimate target of government-authorized confiscation. It necessarily implies that wealth is suspect -- that those who are wealthy owe that wealth, in large measure, to the rest of the country; that, at the discretion of the country, they may be allowed to keep and use it so long as that "works" for society, but that if and when society decides that it needs that wealth to accomplish goals which require more money -- to implement a national healthcare plan, or shrink the deficit, or fund entitlement programs to which the nation has become accustomed -- then society may lay claim to as much of that wealth as it needs to accomplish those goals, and those who earned the wealth will then owe that money to the nation. Obama's fairness argument upends the core presumption of a free economy -- that people are entitled to the wealth they earn by their labor -- in favor of a presumption that wealth, however earned, is a collective resource which may be redistributed at the pleasure of a democratic majority...If we accept the moral presumption that wealth is a collective resource, we surrender a moral premise in favor of private property, the premise which protects all individuals, their labor, and their freedom by rooting those things in the right to earn and to keep their earnings*".

With respect to "fairness" in American taxation, Dr. Walter Williams, a Black economist from George Mason University notes, "*According to Internal Revenue Service data for 2009, the top 1 percent of American income earners paid almost 37 percent of federal income taxes. The top 10 percent paid about 70 percent of federal income taxes, and the top 50 percent paid nearly 98 percent. Roughly 47 percent of Americans pay no federal income tax. Here's my fairness question to you: What standard of fairness dictates that the top 10 percent of income earners pay 70 percent of the income tax burden while 47 percent of Americans pay nothing? The fact that the income tax burden is distributed so unevenly produces great politically borne fiscal problems. People who pay little or no income taxes become natural constituents for big-spending politicians. After all, if you pay no income taxes, what do you care if income taxes are raised? Also, you won't be enthusiastic about tax cuts; you'll see them as a threat to your handouts.*

Regarding equality, the Liberal mindset is more about "inequality", or at least what they perceive to be inequality within our society. That is especially true, in their mind, if one person makes a sum of money larger than another, because somehow that difference in income is an inherent inequality or lack of "liberty" that requires a government redistribution of wealth to correct, no matter if the wealthy person invested in an education and worked twice as hard as another to make that money, or that taking a person's money/property is indeed a form of indenturedness – e.g. slavery. In fact, the Liberal focus on perceived economic inequality is actually at the expense of liberty, because attempting to create equivalence by force of government is of itself its own form of inequality. And, inequality will always be with us, as it is now, even in spite of Liberals having spent around $15T at the federal level over the last 48 years on the so called "War on Poverty", which has resulted in no fewer poor people than it did when it was started.

It is important to note with regards to "equality" that Conservatives believe that all men have the same inalienable rights, but that does not mean that all men should or even could be made equal in all regards, especially by government. In a debate with William Douglas, Abraham Lincoln pointed out that, "*I think the authors of that notable instrument intended to include all men, but they did not mean to declare all men equal in all respects. They did not mean to say all men were equal in color, size, intellect, moral development, or social capacity. They defined with tolerable distinctness in what they did consider all men created equal,—equal in certain inalienable rights, among which are life, liberty, and the pursuit of happiness. This they said, and this they meant. They did not mean to assert the obvious untruth that all were then actually enjoying that equality, or yet that they were about to confer it immediately upon them. In fact, they had no power to confer such a boon. They meant simply to declare the right, so that the enforcement of it might follow as fast as circumstances should permit. They meant to set up a standard maxim for free society which should be familiar to all,—constantly looked to, constantly labored for, and even, though never perfectly attained, constantly approximated, and thereby constantly spreading and deepening its influence, and augmenting the happiness and value of life to all people, of all colors, everywhere.*"

With regards to "justice", Thomas Sowell wrote that, "*The question is not what anybody deserves. The question is who is to take on the God-like role of deciding what everybody else deserves. You can talk about 'social justice' all you want. But what death taxes boil down to is letting politicians take money from widows and orphans to pay for goodies that they will hand out to others, in order to buy votes to get re-elected. That is not social justice or any other kind of justice*". After all, to be true, justice must have many faces, thus faithfully representing all factions, individuals and viewpoints, not just one man or one viewpoint at the expense of another – a dissonant viewpoint that is frightfully championed by Liberals, no different in many ways than their segregationist forefathers.

22 THE DANGEROUS LIBERAL DEMAGOGUERY OF FELLOW AMERICANS

Starting especially with Ronald Reagan, but occurring even well before that, Liberals have used the most vile personal attacks and name calling as their primary weapon of choice in their attempts to silence other Americans –those who have different political viewpoints. This practice has gotten much worse under Obama, extending even to very dangerous levels.

The favorite Liberal tactic in the 1980' and 1990's was to denigrate Conservatives/Republicans by questioning their intelligence and calling them "stupid" (e.g., Ronald Reagan, Dan Quale), but when George W. Bush ran against Al Gore for president, this tactic backfired because, as it turned out, Bush had a much better academic record than did Gore. As a result, the Liberal rhetoric started to become more strident, more hateful and more dangerous – dangerous because it incited some to commit criminal acts against the life and property of other Americans. These unconscionable acts by Liberals were favorite tactics of the Clintons, but have become even worse under Obama. They are carried out primarily by the faithful minions of Liberalism, including the sycophantic MSM (main stream media), which faithfully and blindly repeats "talking points" given to them under the table by the Obama administration.

In his blog entitled "Liberalism's Willing Executioners", about how genocide under the Nazis was undertaken by "countless thousands and millions of ordinary Germans, Paul Kengor writes, "*What the American Left has done to its enemies is not entirely dissimilar, even while certainly not [yet] approaching the crass, deadly level of the Nazis. But whether it's Obama himself, or his campaign, or Media Matters or MoveOn.org or any number of left-wing groups and websites and publications and media outlets, the American Left has been merciless in thoroughly demonizing opponents. Liberals don't just politely disagree, or agree that people can disagree; no -- too often they caricature those who disagree as vile reprobates with no possible good intentions or reasoning for their positions. It's a very illiberal thing to do.*

Kengor also writes, "*Take the Tea Party, for starters. Once they saw the Tea Party's effectiveness, especially after the 2010 midterm elections, liberals/"progressives" went on a rampage, smearing the wide swath of Tea Party members (whom they probably never met) as recalcitrant racists. It was a charge totally unfair and ludicrous. I know people in the Tea Party. I watched the group develop. They are absolutely not racists; they were driven completely by the fiscal madness of Obama and the Pelosi Democratic Congress in the first six months of Obama's presidency. But once liberals starting ramping up their crude caricature, with congressmen and NPR executives and respected left-wing journals of opinion like the New York Times leading the way, the liberal mob responded in kind. Tea Party members were labeled as the worst kind of "extremists."*

The result was shocking to behold. Like wildfire, liberals/progressives everywhere were swept up, fuming with anger and fanning the flames. They mimicked the party line without any question whatsoever. They whipped themselves into an emotional frenzy, convinced with absolute righteousness that this insidious group of racists was trying to undermine the saintly, kindly Obama for no reason other than the color of his skin.

As conservatives, we saw from the outset that this was pure politics -- actually, pure political demagoguery. Conservative talk-shows played clips from select liberals (such as Chuck Schumer) admitting as much. We saw right through it. But liberals don't think that way. They aren't wired that way. They're incredibly emotional people who can be easily prodded by their party/ideological elite, especially with the spontaneity and instant communication of social media -- the new mother's milk of the liberal mob. They really are prone to fads and fashions and mass behavior in ways that conservatives plainly aren't. I've seen it again and again. Conservatives aren't perfect, and have their own quirks and vices, but they don't tend toward this kind of group thinking and collective action. For conservatives, the ability to think logically and independently, based upon beliefs and values deeper and timeless, and to not be seduced by what Pope Benedict XVI calls the "anonymous power" of the latest fads and fashions, is what makes them conservative to begin with.

And so, when word was out among the Left that the Tea Party was comprised of genuine evildoers, the wider liberal masses, whether at blogs and nonprofits and Facebook or working for the IRS not only responded; they retaliated. They acted naturally. They didn't need Obama to tell them what to do. Exactly as Herb Meyer says, there was never any need for a printed order from Obama.

Tea Party aside, the American Left is also viciously targeting those who dare to oppose gay marriage. Here, too, liberals/progressives refuse to agree to disagree. Those who stand for traditional marriage as people have understood it since the literal dawn of humanity are framed as awful people, as intolerant "haters," almost subhuman in their lack of compassion. They are a form of modern American untermesnchen, utterly despised -- contemptible.

When an Oregon couple, a baker and his wife, declined to make a wedding cake for two members of the same sex, the apostles of tolerance and diversity went screaming mad, attacking the couple with profanities and threatening lawsuits -- with no respect at all for the couples' freedom. "You stupid bible thumping, hypocritical [expletive]," wrote one loving liberal in an email. "I hope your kids get really, really, sick and you go out of business." Another champion of compassion added: "Here's hoping you go out of business, you bigot. Enjoy hell."

Organizations trying to stop gay marriage -- that is, trying to stop the redefinition of marriage, and believe that children need a mom and a dad -- are being derided as "hate groups."

A near-tragic example happened with the Family Research Council, which was labeled a "hate group." I know people at the Family Research Council. They are good-hearted, classic social conservatives. Their social positions aren't different from where the Democratic Party stood for over a century.

But once an organization of "civil rights" liberals labeled the Family Research Council a "hate group," the charge went viral, and then, one fateful day last August, an enraged homosexual activist headed for the group's offices with an arsenal of bullets and weapons poorly concealed in Chick-fil-A bags. He was stopped only by an alert security guard, who was shot and injured.

This left-wing gay activist, convinced that the Family Research Council was promulgating "hate," was prompted to an act of attempted mass murder.

This example should be widely known. It isn't. Why not? Because the mainstream media hasn't made it a national issue. If this had been a conservative shooter targeting a liberal organization, with a conservative president in the White House, all of conservatism would be held complicit, and the media would demand the president condemn the action. There would be a national media campaign against "conservative extremism."

Speaking of Chick-fil-A, it, too, has been a target of leftist rage: boycotts, protests, pickets, mayors of big cities trying to ban the restaurant and describing its product as "hate chicken." Why? Simply because the CEO is against gay marriage, which not long ago was the position of Bill and Hillary Clinton and the entire Democratic Party.

Beyond Chick-fil-A, look at the Left's Occupy Wall Street brigades. Here again, there was no edict from Barack Obama or David Axelrod to organize these people. Nonetheless, plenty of incessant Obama demonization of "profits," corporate "jet-owners," nefarious "millionaires and billionaires," big banks, big oil, those not paying their "fair share," and, of course, the monsters on "Wall Street," did the trick. The "progressive" mob sprang into action. In no time, they were marching not only on Wall Street but on front lawns of corporate CEOs -- a very volatile situation.

And then there's the hideous charge that Republicans who oppose mandatory taxpayer funding of abortion somehow thus favor a "war on women." Sandra Fluke has become a liberal heroine for that cultural/political obscenity.

In sum, these leftists are Obama's and (more widely) liberalism's willing executioners. They obviously aren't literally executing people -- although that was indeed the literal intent of the Family Research Council gunman -- but they are executing what they believe is a glorious plan for the fundamental transformation of America. They are willingly executing Obama's agenda and their agenda. Any opponents are isolated as enemies and maligned in the most demeaning way.

And what does this mean? Among other things, it means that liberals really do need to be damned careful about what they're doing here. There are seriously disturbing consequences to their systematic demonization of anyone who disagrees with them. This is becoming truly dangerous. Lives and careers will be destroyed."

This level of hateful demagoguery by Liberals against their fellow Americans has become especially noticeable recently, as Obama's minions are now out in force supporting his insane carbon tax policies in a hateful way by publishing lists of Senators and Congressmen (Conservatives) that do not support these policies. These missives describe people who do not believe in anthropogenic global warming as "deniers" and suggest that they are deniers due to limited intelligence. Also, Obama and his administration have recently more and more expressed their opinions publicly that Conservatives and Tea Party members are more dangerous to America than are Islamic terrorists!

Unfortunately, due to the now accepted (by Liberals) use of Gestapo-like hate tactics against other Americans, political discourse in America has reached such a low level of civility it can be argued that the country is lost politically. In the meantime, you will hear Liberals lie and obfuscate that it is Conservatives who are engaging in hate speech, but nothing is further from the truth. Especially more and more strident recently is the Liberal hateful rhetoric that is being used against those who believe in the Constitution – Conservatives. This cognitive dissonant anger of Liberalism is now on full display and Liberals are destroying the country with their malicious hatred.

23 A LIMITED FEDERAL GOVERNMENT – WHY?

Why do Conservatives agree with America's Founders regarding keeping the government limited - one of the people, by the people and for the people - whereas Liberals seem willing to give up everything for a larger and larger government, including giving up all of our precious liberties and freedoms and even our lives?

First it is important to note that most attempts at "social reform", or Obama's "hope and change", have historically been rooted in Marxist socialist philosophies of big centralized governments with their primary goal the creation of a "perfect society" and secondly that all have failed miserably over time, even to the extent of creating mass starvation (Africa, China), mass genocide (Germany, Russia, China) and the complete destruction and (or) dehumanization of the very societies the Leftists were trying to "perfect". In fact the Greeks actually invented democracy to get away from large centralized government, recognizing its limitations and threats. And, our American Founders, in complete understanding and recognition of these threats, developed what is without a doubt the best system of government in the world and that is the American form of a limited federal government, with limited power and numerous checks and balances against the abuse of power, so that that power could never be used against the people - as long as the Constitution is adhered to. The limitations on power are necessary, because as said best by British historian Lord Acton, "*Power tends to corrupt, and absolute power corrupts absolutely.*"

Daren Jonescu writes, "*Hence the case for limited government, and the rule of law. For those educated in public schools, the word "limited" in that first phrase means "limited in power." The purpose of such a foundational principle is not to cast aspersions on the integrity of any particular man in government, but rather to acknowledge a sobering fact of life, which is that we are all, in principle, morally susceptible to the temptations presented by the opportunity for perceived personal advantage gained without fear of retribution. Thus, although government is a useful and necessary instrument for protecting life, property, and civil order, and therefore an aid in the pursuit of virtue and happiness -- or rather, precisely because it is such a necessary and useful instrument -- a governing authority that becomes too expansive in its capability to control and manipulate the population from which it derives its purpose loses its legitimacy*"

Further Jonescu writes, "*Then there is the further problem of the dispersal of such tempting power among an enormous group of largely anonymous agents. It is one thing to give a king, a president, or an elected congress more power than is safe in the hands of flawed men. But the tendency of modern authority -- a tendency which is almost definitive of what we have come to call "totalitarianism"-- is for excessive powers from the top to filter down through an unwieldy and increasingly unaccountable bureaucracy. At present, untold numbers of low-level operatives, computer specialists, and what not, have "legal" tools at their disposal that can intrude upon your private actions and associations against your will, and without your knowledge. The words "national security" name an important function of legitimate government, but they are neither a talisman against personal corruption, nor a magic password justifying the "unlimiting" of government. National security," used as such a magic password, is no different, in principle, from so many other magic passwords used in modern times to justify unreasonable expansions of state authority, such as "affordable healthcare," "fairness," "the children," "equal opportunity," "social justice," and so on.*"

Our founding fathers wrote in the Declaration of Independence, "*That to secure these rights, governments are instituted among men, deriving their just powers from the consent of the governed. That whenever any form of government becomes destructive to these ends, it is the right of the people to alter or to abolish it, and to institute new government, laying its foundation on such principles and organizing its powers in such form, as to them shall seem most likely to effect their safety and happiness. Prudence, indeed, will dictate that governments long established should not be changed for light and transient causes; and accordingly all experience hath shown that mankind are more disposed to suffer, while evils are sufferable, than to right themselves by abolishing the forms to which they are accustomed. But when a long train of abuses and usurpations, pursuing invariably the same object evinces a design to reduce them under absolute despotism, it is their right, it is their duty, to throw off such government, and to provide new guards for their future security.*"

In a true cognitive dissonance, Liberals simply do not understand the threats that unlimited governments pose, even in spite of the recent Obama scandals that clearly highlight such abuses.

24 ILLEGAL IMMIGRATION

The Liberal practice of selectively upholding the rule of law in America is highlighted most by illegal immigration, where every illegal immigrant first must break the country's laws to gain entry. This is especially evident by Obama refusing to do his sworn duty to uphold federal immigration law by not prosecuting immigration crime, thus compounding two crimes – one of illegal entry with one of illegal residence. According to the Liberal mindset, we cannot call people who enter the country unlawfully "illegal aliens", rather we must refer to them as "undocumented workers", further removing the concept of legality from the process and letting the Liberal off the hook with regards to the the rule of law in America. Never mind that the legal definition of alien is, "*A foreigner, esp. one who is not a naturalized citizen of the country where they are living*" and the country of Mexico has some of the most stringent immigration laws in the world, including "*Foreigners who are deported from Mexico and attempt to re-enter the country without authorization can be imprisoned for up to 10 years. Foreigners who violate the terms of their visa may be sentenced to up to six years in prison. Foreigners who misrepresent the terms of their visa while in Mexico — such as working without a permit — can also be imprisoned*" Liberals ignore Mexico's highly punitive immigration laws, and in fact one of the greatest dichotomies on earth are Mexicans who complain about US immigration laws, while at the same time supporting their own county's draconian laws.

Conservatives believe in the rule of law, and thus we believe that illegal immigration is precisely what it is – the illegal breaking of our nation's laws to gain entry. With what has to be recognized as one of the greatest transgressions in history by a US president, Obama not only ignores the rule of law regarding illegal immigration, he has actually brought federal lawsuits against states that desire to protect their economies and citizens from the harmful impact of illegal immigration. A perhaps even worse, Liberals argue that illegal immigrants should be afforded all of the social benefits that citizens have a right to, at a tremendous cost to the states. In California alone, the total cost for illegal immigrants is estimated to be approximately $22 B per year. It was estimated by the Heritage Foundation recently that the cost of the recent immigration bill, in which an estimated 11 million illegal immigrants would be given a path to legal residence including government social benefits, would be at least $6 T, an unconscionable amount. And this bill has now reached 1,000 pages in length, with who knows what in it – similar to Obamacare.

The problem of illegal immigration in the US falls squarely at the feet of the federal government, which has done nothing about it. But, why is this? It is because Democrats are fully aware that illegal immigrants from Mexico tend to vote for Democrats, so they and their complicit media support illegal immigration to increase their power – something that they should all be impeached for. Ed Lasky points out that due to the dramatic decline in the populations of the major cities in the US, which are almost exclusively Democrat strongholds, "*Democrats in the largest cities of L.A., Chicago, and New York sponsor illegal immigration in order to save public sector union jobs and congressional seats. But illegal immigrants are largely funded through Federal programs. These program dollars create debt for all voters. Then the newspapers and TV news outlets in Chicago can't discuss the huge public debt, since it will make Democrats look bad, and hurt their own demographics. The Illinois public sector pension debt was exposed by the Illinois Better Government Association and Illinois Policy Institute. It was not researched by the big papers and TV stations. This debt continues to be grown by illegal immigration. So as the media ignore the great scheme of corruption they create more debt for the middle class and poor throughout the country. All because media want to protect their own "media market" turf and keep the population propped up.*" This "sponsorship" of illegal immigration includes the development of "sanctuary cities" which is just an acronym for the illegal practice of ignoring federal immigration law

Conservatives believe that to stop the illegal immigration problem, we should first protect our borders and then, after having done so, have a civil public discourse on how to deal with the people who reside illegally in our country, perhaps offering them a path to citizenship only after paying fines and taking the citizen tests required of every legal immigrant, with no government benefits for at least 15 years.

The other underreported problem with Liberal policies is legal immigration. As a result of Ted Kennedy's Immigration Reform Act of 1965, the level of immigration increased from approximately 250,000 to approximately 1,000,000 per year. And, even more importantly, America's immigration policies changed from bringing in the best and brightest from other countries, people who help shape America into what it is today, to allowing 85 percent of our new arrivals to hail from the 3rd world and Asia. This radical departure from America's traditional immigration patterns has created not only huge demographic changes, but also tremendous social and cost impacts.

25 THE INSANITY OF THE LEFT

From out-of-control government spending, due to unsustainable socialist promises, to all aspects of government and politics, including an outright disdain for the founding principles of our country, the insanity of the Left and of Liberals is so enormous in its breadth and scope as to be almost impossible for us Conservatives to comprehend or to describe. In a true form of cognitive dissonance, somehow in American politics we have gone from truth and honor being a political strength to lying and deceit being not only acceptable but honorable to Liberals and to the Left. And worse yet, there are Americans in our society who believe in, and even defend, the obfuscations and lies told to them by Democrat politicians, including accepting polar opposites even in the same sentence. It is as if two philosophies were involved in a head on collision – a collision between rational thought and deceit, between right and wrong – with the end result being that all aspects of truth and honor died on impact and "the end justifies the means" became, at least to the Left, the only surviving guiding principle.

Examples of Liberal cognitive dissonances are too numerous to describe in detail but especially include their attitude towards the nation's voting laws. The absolute fact is that in America today you cannot do anything without personal identification; you have to present ID to go to a bar, to buy cigarettes, to cash a check, to use a credit card, to see a physician, to go to the hospital, to drive a car, to get married, or even to open a bank account, to name a few. As well, most states have laws that if you do not have an ID in your possession you can be considered a vagrant and thrown in jail. Yet, Liberals argue the insane position that people should not have to present personal identification to vote. This crazy stance, now supported by the Liberal Supreme Court, has nothing whatsoever with "disenfranchising" voters, as they try to lead you to believe, because it could be argued we are "disenfranchising" everyone from American society, due to the endless requirements for ID. Rather, what they are in fact fighting for, without admitting to it publicly, is to make voter fraud by the Left easy to accomplish. This is in direct contradiction to their stated public position regarding the importance and sanctity of "one man, one vote" in America. Of course, even more in contradiction to preserving voter sanctity is the recent IRS scandal, in which the Leftist government under Obama illegally used the IRS to suppress the Conservative Tea Party vote during the 2012 presidential election.

Other examples of the insanity of the Left are detailed below:

- Barney Frank, "*We would have unemployment below 8% if it weren't for the fact that Republicans have forced cities and states to lay off 700,000 people.*"
- Harry Belafonte's recent advice to Obama, "*To imprison opposition,*" - without due process and like a third world dictator.
- Jeff Spross, "*Extending unemployment benefits creates five times as many jobs per dollar of budget deficit as the Bush income tax cuts for the wealthy.*"
- Obama 2011 Jobs Bill, "*Employers can be sued for discrimination if they don't hire a person that is unemployed.*"
- Obama, "*Extending unemployment insurance will create more jobs than the Keystone Pipeline.*"
- New law in California invokes, "*A $1,000 fine for people ignoring a new prohibition against 'any person to cast, toss, throw, kick or roll any object other than a beach ball or a volley ball upon or over any beach between Memorial Day and Labor Day'.*" So, if you want to throw a football or a Frisbee – don't!
- Time report, "*East Coast Blizzard Tied to Climate Change*", vis-à-vis Robert F. Kennedy's column, "*Anemic Winters in the Washington Area Tied to Climate Change.*"
- California, "*Four high-school students suspended for chanting 'USA' at a school sporting event.*"
- Chris Mathews, "*Obama rivals are like 'secessionists' who want to kill him.*" Chris, but weren't the southern secessionists and the KKK almost exclusively Democrats?
- British scientists, "*Giant dinosaurs could have warmed the climate with their flatulence.*"
- Human Services Secretary Kathleen Sebelius, "*…told students they could do a lot of good by telling some students they were 'jerks, immediately after showing a video that admonishes children not to call people names like 'stupid, 'fat' and 'jerk'.*"
- US teacher, "*Cries 'hate crime' over Bible being left on her desk.*"
- Fort Worth, "*High school student suspended when he told classmates 'I'm Christian and, to me, homosexuality is wrong.*"
- Baltimore, "*A 7–year old student was suspended because a teacher thought he was modeling a Pop-tart he was nibbling on into the shape of a gun.*"
- Maryland, "*First grader suspended for making gun gesture with finger.*"
- "*A Michigan elementary school is defending its decision to confiscate a third-graders batch of homemade cupcakes because the birthday treats were decorated with plastic green Army soldiers.*"

- Governor Pat Quinn, "…*sometimes I wonder if I would make a concession for the death penalty when it comes to gun owners.*" So, let's see "Pat", there are at least an estimated 52 million households in the US that own guns, so if we just kill one person out of the household, are we going to kill 52 million Americans for owning guns, or should we just kill all 145.6 million, including the kids?
- Audrey Gibson, a Democrat Senator, recently filed a bill in Florida that would, "…*require anyone trying to buy ammunition to first complete an anger management course, and to do so every ten years.*" I guess that we sportsmen are "angry" at our prey and paper targets?
- A domestic organization only, the TSA, "*In 2012, purchased 1.4 billion rounds of mostly hollow point frangible ammunition, or approximately five rounds for every person in the country.*" This is while, "*The Hague Convention of 1899, Declaration III, prohibited the use in international warfare of bullets that easily expand or flatten in the body.*"

Need I continue? Sadly, these kinds of quotes regarding the dissonances of irrational cognitions of the Left in America could go on for hundreds of pages…

26 NATIONAL PRIDE

In a true perversion of rational thought, the Marxist Gore Vidal in a debate with William F. Buckley in the early 1960's was among the first to call Conservatives "Nazis". This perversion has been used since by Liberals in government and elsewhere more and more recently, including in 2009 when Nancy Pelosi referred to people who were against government sponsored healthcare as "Nazis" and Al Gore used the same term to denigrate scientists who do not agree with man-caused global warming.

However, the party of Hitler was actually the National Socialist German Workers Party (NSDAP), which promoted extreme left wing socialist ideals. In direct contradiction to this fact, even in tomes such as Wikipedia, the Nazi Party today is mistakenly correlated with a right wing movement, because of one thing – the Nazis were strong nationalists. And, as such, nationalism has been associated with Conservative principles by some. But, if nationalism is truly a Conservative ideal, one so fundamental as to allow the categorization of the socialist leftist Nazis as being "right wing", then by extension the left wing must not be nationalistic, even in spite of the fact that many modern socialistic societies have become nationalist socialists, such as in Cuba, Venezuela, Argentina and France.

It is true that Conservatives are proud to be Americans and believe in American exceptionalism, and thus could be called nationalistic. However, we prefer to think of ourselves as being patriotic. Conversely, many Liberals in America are vehemently anti American.

Conservatives believe that for a country to be united and to flourish, its citizenry should be proud of its own country. And in America there is so very much to be proud of. So while people like Obama spend time apologizing for America, and are rarely if ever heard talking about American exceptionalism, Conservatives are unabashedly patriotic and believe in American exceptionalism. Lately, a Liberal professor from an eastern US Ivy League school referred to the 4th of July as a "Conservative holiday" attended only by "beer drinking, gun toting Republicans" – a holiday that should warrant no Liberal participation. This is the thinking of many on the Left, but if so then Conservatives are happy to be the only ones who celebrate that on July 4, 1776 the Declaration of Independence was adopted, giving birth both to American independence and to the beginnings of this great nation.

27 RACISM

In keeping with the main tenants of the Constitution, Conservatives strongly believe that all men are created equal, that racism is abhorrent and to deprive someone of their property and their labor on the basis of race, or for any other reason, is wrong. Because we are vehemently against racism, we also believe that reverse racism is just as bad and just as wrong. Liberals on the other hand strongly support government mandated racist policies, such as affirmative action. They are quick to label, with their politics of hate, all Conservatives as racist. But there is nothing further from the truth.

The fight against slavery was waged by Abraham Lincoln, the first Republican president. And, after the 13th Amendment, the most important piece of anti-discrimination legislation was the Civil Rights Act of 1964. While this legislation was first called for by John F. Kennedy, a Democrat (and a Conservative), its passage was largely due to Republican support, with a majority of the dissenters being southern Democrats, who were vehement segregationists. In fact, in direct contradiction to what the Left will have you believe, the southern KKK was almost exclusively comprised of Democrats and it was Democrats who mostly opposed the Civil Rights Act (they were also against the anti-slavery 13th Amendment and against women's suffrage).

To illustrate how far the Liberals in our American universities have gone in terms of promoting divisiveness and hate in America based on race, in November 2007 the University of Delaware made a decision to "*subject its students to mandatory 'treatment' where they learn[ed] that 'all whites are racist,' racism by 'people of color' is impossible, and George Washington is merely a 'famous Indian fighter, large landholder and slave holder.*" The young students at the university were told the following in a clear attempt to indoctrinate those young people with a twisted Liberal ideology (Note: this case is just one of many.):

A RACIST: A racist is one who is both privileged and socialized on the basis of race by a white supremacist (racist) system. The term applies to all white people (i.e., people of European descent) living in the United States, regardless of class, gender, religion, culture or sexuality. By this definition, people of color cannot be racists, because as peoples within the system, they do not have the power to back up their prejudices, hostilities, or acts of discrimination [.]

REVERSE RACISM: A term created and used by white people to deny their white privilege. Those in denial use the term reverse racism to refer to hostile behavior by people of color toward whites, and to affirmative action policies, which allegedly give 'preferential treatment' to people of color over whites.

Some people in American understand all of this. Recently, State Sen. Elbert Guillory, a Black senator from Louisiana, explained his reasons for leaving the Democrat party and switching to the Republican Party, citing Democrat opposition to civil rights, their attitudes toward people and their desire for "control." He said, "*The black community, which he invited to join him in the move, should quit exchanging self-reliance for the "allegiance of overseers" through government programs that are intended not to help people, but to control them.* Also, "*those Democrats push a social justice and welfare aid strategy to manage citizens, not help them from poverty… In recent history, the Democratic Party has created the illusion that their agenda and their policies are what's best for black people. Somehow, it has been forgotten that the Republican Party was founded in 1854 as an abolitionist movement, with one simple creed – that slavery is a violation of the rights of man.*" He also noted it was Republicans who pushed for the 13th, 14th and 15th Amendments giving Blacks citizenship, voting rights and due process. "*Democrats, on the other hand, were the party of Jim Crow. It was the Democrats who defended the rights of slave owners. At the heart of liberalism is the idea that only a great and powerful big government can be the benefactor of social justice for all Americans. But the left is only concerned with one thing: control. And they disguise this control as charity.*"

We Conservatives hope that all Americans are against all forms of racism and the concept that only Liberals are against racism, while Conservatives are all racists, and that racism is confined only to white people is one of the greatest lies and twisted perversions perpetrated by the Left in this country. In fact, as stated by Senator Guillory the opposite is really true, where Liberals enslave mostly minorities into a life of socioeconomic submission with their welfare policies. And, keeping the many faces of racism alive is actually necessary for Liberals to succeed, even as America has led the world in racial reform. It is a fact that the Liberal "business model" is built around antagonizing blacks into believing that race relations in America are still stuck in the 19th century, so that they will vote for them, and attempting to use race against Conservatives wherever possible, simply because in the eyes of some if you are called a "racist" you are guilty as charged without due consideration.

If we really look "under the dress" of Liberalism when it comes to racism, we will see a shocking fact. In America today, 76% of black children are born out of wedlock, the youth unemployment rate in 2013 was 40.9% for blacks, a rate double that for whites, and black youths have a 29% chance of spending time in prison compared to only 4% for whites. These are real statistics that illustrate real problems, but none of this is talked about by Liberals or dealt with, or even worse yet by Obama, a Black man, because they are proof that Liberal policies over the last 50 years have been both racist and abject failures. It is truly a sad fact that the Liberal ideology has helped destroy American black people and other minorities. Yet, according to Liberals, Conservatives are not allowed to be part of the debate regarding these failures, because to do so is "racist" and according to them no failures actually exist. I submit the opposite. That to not understand these problems and to not re-evaluate America's social policies in light of modern real world outcomes is in itself institutionalized racism, and all Americans, irrespective of race, should be aware of how Liberals have both fostered racial divides and hurt minorities in America with their socialist, racist government policies.

The promotion of racial divisions in America by Liberals has many ugly faces but it also has tremendous potential negative consequences for all Americans. Especially as promoted by Obama and the Left recently, you are automatically guilty if you are white. Instead of the rule of law being the face of justice in America, racial rhetoric has become our new "trial by jury" – where instead of justice being served people are found guilty publicaly by a biased jury of Liberal haters, no matter their true innocence or guilt. Examples of this include the Duke Lacrosse team and George Zimmerman, where even when these people were found innocent by trial, there continued to be chilling threats against their lives due to the racial hatred stirred up by the Left.

Conservatives believe that the federal government should have a limited role in the race "business", with its only responsibility being to provide laws and legislation that ensure equal access to all to our nation's institutions and organizations. But, with the civil rights legislation that has already been passed and is on the books, equal access already has already been guaranteed. It is not the responsibility of government, nor should it be permitted, to try to force equal outcomes, to in any way favor one group of people over another and (or) to attempt to right perceived past wrongs, irrespective of race, gender or income level. Giving a clear example to the racial dichotomies that exist in America today, the Supreme Court recently admitted for the first time that affirmative action "trammels the rights" of many citizens, but then proceeded to call it "constitutional".

28 SAME-SEX MARRIAGE

Marriage is a social institution created for the most part as a legal structure to track the inheritance of property and ancestry from generation to generation. In no society is marriage a codified right in law, as opposed to what the Left will lead you to believe. Marriage between a man and a woman is therefore necessary to give a legal structure to that union, within a societal structure, and inherent in the practice of marriage is the presumption that the union will evolve/continue through having offspring – children. Different constructs of ancestry/marriage have been used through time, including many early matriarchal societies where ancestry was only tracked through the female. As well, polygamy is still practiced in some countries today. But, irrespective of the archeological history of ancestry, the standard for such unions now in America and in much of the world is that marriage is between one man and one woman. This is first and foremost a societal construct to ensure a legal structure for the progression of progeny and inheritance.

In an article by Dominique Ludvigson, he writes:

> *"In the vast majority of states, marriage is still defined as between one man and one woman by statute, state constitutional amendment, or both. Where the question has been put directly to the people of the states, they have overwhelmingly supported retaining this definition of marriage. For instance:*
>
> *Under the laws of 42 states, marriage remains defined as the union of a man and a woman.*
>
> *Citizens have voted for this definition of marriage in every state where they have been given the opportunity to do so—32 states in all.*
>
> *In 30 of these states, marriage between one man and one woman is constitutionally protected, thereby precluding the legislature and state courts from redefining the institution without the people's consent. North Carolina became the 30th state to pass a constitutional amendment retaining the definition of marriage between one man and one woman in May of this year. Its voters approved the amendment by a wide margin: 61 percent to 39 percent. In addition, Hawaii's constitution reserves the question of marriage to the legislature, which voted to retain the traditional definition of marriage, and voters in Maine supported a ballot measure in 2009 that repealed a bill redefining marriage that was passed by the legislature.*
>
> *Marriage has never been redefined by a referendum of the people in any state".*

While marriage is an integral part of the Christian religious belief, it is also a secular construct, as marriages in America may be performed by a Justice of the Peace. That this construct may evolve in the future is not of importance to the issue at hand. People who claim to be religious in one form or another make up about 73% of the US population and most of these folks, as well as many others, are against homosexual marriage. Because where will that type of union lead? The argument already being made by some is if homosexual marriage is acceptable, how can you discriminate against polygamy or polyandry? And, what if a person wants to "marry" their pet? This has already been proposed and is not as outlandish a possibility as it sounds. Or how about "marrying" children?

Once society goes down the path of "anything is acceptable because it is a "right", "*especially if they successfully argue their version of marriage on utilitarian grounds -- it benefits or does no harm to society*", then there are no bounds and the structure of our society falls apart, with real consequences to the traditional family structure, combined with the documented consequence of increased crime, poverty and lassitude. So for you Liberals, who want to embrace any "progressive" concept that comes along, at least try to think of what the short and long term consequences to society are. However, I seriously doubt such rational inspection will ever enter your mind, as your Liberal ideology does not allow you to think about the impact on others - on families, on children and on our entire society.

Liberals would rather advocate for a man marrying a man than they would for heterosexual marriage, where more and more children in America are being born out of wedlock, especially in Black families, with all of the consequences involved – poverty, crime and poor educational outcomes - setting those children on course for a life of misery and despair. But I forgot; in the mind of a Liberal, children have no rights.

29 UTOPIAN SOCIETY

In 1516, Sir Thomas Moore, while describing Utopia in the context of an idealized perfect place, coined the term Utopia from the Greek: οὐ, "not", and τόπος, "place"", indicating that he was utilizing the concept as allegory; and, as such, he did not consider such an ideal place to be realistically possible. But the entire Liberal ideology has been described by many as a desire to create a Liberal Utopian society in America. The foundations of this concept actually come from socialist and communist principles advanced in part by Marx and Engels. But, what is wrong with these Liberal Utopian ideals, and why is the concept of creating a Utopia in America so misguided, if not actually outright dangerous?

The fundamental problem with trying to create a Liberal Utopia, or any other kind of Utopia in America, or in any other country for that matter, is that every man and women is happy under a different set of changing circumstances and conditions. One person's Utopia may well be another person's hell. For example, one person may be happier working, learning and growing (a Conservative), while another may be the most happy doing nothing at all for himself or for anyone else (a Liberal). To then force the concept of a Liberal Utopia on society, by worshipping diversity while actually trying to force equal outcomes, is a concept that is both doomed to failure and one that is abhorrent to Conservatives.

As an example of how Liberals see the world differently from Conservatives, and how diametrically opposed their Utopia would be compared to others, Oleg Atbashian, a writer from the former USSR, recently wrote, "*From the economy to crime prevention to education to foreign relations, America's policies today are based on the Marxist premise that crime results from poverty, economic crisis results from greed, injustice results from capitalist exploitation, corruption results from the free markets, and militant Islamism results from Western colonialism. Therefore, peace and harmony can only be achieved through equal redistribution of wealth, appeasement, and a global effort to reshape human nature through politically correct, collectivist indoctrination.*

Liberals have a collective Utopian view of the world, rather than believing in liberty and individualism, and that is why they are trying to force their ideas of a Utopian society on others - a Utopia they dream of where "*the human mind is a "social construct" shaped entirely by manipulation and social conditioning*". But, that Utopia is not one that many truly would be happy being part of, according to Conservative principles, because we believe the exact opposite, that "... *our individual thoughts, motives, and actions are governed, for the most part, by absolute moral standards, which are objectively derived from the unchangeable nature of human beings and the nature of the world.*"

Liberal utopianism, better referred to as "cultism", or "cultural Marxism", is really about control, rather than it is about freedom, where Liberals believe in using the government to force their ideals on others. These are extreme and dangerous viewpoints, because first and foremost the question must be asked, who will define the Liberal Utopian paradigm? And, secondly, who then will decide what is good for each and every one of us – government bureaucrats and Liberal radicals? These viewpoints are dangerous because they represent a collectivist creed supported by an amoral dogma designed to force a single corrupt ideology on all of the people, no matter the dreams of the individuals involved, their aspirations, or the outcome of their true happiness.

Conservatives believe that people are happiest in a free society, where they have the liberty and self determination to pursue their own goals and their own contentment - where happiness comes from creativity, growth, and wellbeing. And, the only country in the world in which the people are truly free and empowered to pursue their own dreams is in America -at least for now.

30 PUBLIC DEBT FROM A HISTORIC PERSPECTIVE

Conservatives very strongly believe that all governments have an obligation to the people to be fiscally responsible, because, as stated by Thomas Jefferson, "*And to preserve their independence, we must not let our rulers load us with perpetual debt. We must make our election between economy and liberty, or profusion and servitude… This example reads to us the salutary lesson, that private fortunes are destroyed by public as well as by private extravagances. And this is the tendency of all human governments. A departure from principle in one instance becomes a precedent for the second; that second for a third; and so on, till the bulk of the society is reduced to mere automatons of misery, to have no sensibilities left but for sinning and suffering. Then begins, indeed, the bellum omnium in omnia, which some philosophers observing to be so general in this world, have mistaken for the natural, instead of the abusive state of man. And the fore horse on this frightful team is public debt. Taxation follows that, and in its train wretchedness and oppression.*"

Also with regard to public debt, as Ludwig von Mise wrote the following:

> "*It is important to remember that government interference always means either violent action or the threat of such action. The funds that a government spends for whatever purposes are levied by taxation. And taxes are paid because the taxpayers are afraid of offering resistance to the tax gatherers. They know that any disobedience or resistance is hopeless. As long as this is the state of affairs, the government is able to collect the money that it wants to spend. Government is in the last resort the employment of armed men… Those who are asking for more government interference are asking ultimately for more compulsion and less freedom.*"

This is not to suggest that Conservatives do not believe in any form of taxation – to have a functioning government that government must have the ability to raise funds to fulfill the obligations for which it was created. And, the 16th Amendment gives the power to the federal government to collect an income tax. But to destroy the future of America with frightful government debt, by promising non Constitution-based programs that can never be paid for, is not only abhorrent, it is directly contrary to why the federal government was established by the people to begin with, which is as stated in the Preamble to the Constitution, "*We the people of the United States, in order to form a more perfect union, establish justice, insure domestic tranquility, provide for the common defense, promote the general welfare, and secure the blessings of liberty to ourselves and our posterity, do ordain and establish this Constitution for the United States of America*".

The official federal debt is $16 trillion and now represents 100% of the country's GDP. Historically, it has been shown that debts near GDP have a significant impact on growth – they hurt both the economy of the country and in turn the wellbeing of its people. However, as will be pointed out elsewhere, $16 T is actually the government's own accounting of that debt. The real US debt from other liabilities, including Treasury obligations from other government agencies such as Freddie Mac and Fannie Mae ($6T.) and other unfunded liabilities (from $50 T to $200 T) amounts to ~$11 T per year, not the $1.3 T presently reported, if US standard accounting procedures (GAAP accounting) were to be used instead of the government's own accounting methods. This extreme debt is not only unsustainable; it is heading America towards bankruptcy and ruin, all as a result of Liberal policies.

Very importantly, the people of America must begin to recognize the tremendous threat that our combined debts pose to our future and to vociferously stand against them. And, by extension, anyone is this country who does not recognize these threats and who do not stand against them are not only complicit in the country's destruction, but they also will be participating in their own ruin and in their children's diminished futures. As Thomas Jefferson famously said, "*It is incumbent on every generation to pay its own debts as it goes. A principle which if acted on would save one-half the wars of the world.*" But, the Left is vehemently in support of out-of-control government spending. To Conservatives, this is the truest form of public greed; and government debt, coupled with this greed, is undoubtedly the greatest threat this nation and others face.

31 MODERN ECONOMICS AND THE GREED OF THE LEFT

Why the Democrat Party has moved so far to the left, so very far away from the founding ideals of this great nation, to an outright unqualified support of socialism coupled with redistributive philosophy, higher taxation and logarithmically increasing government regulation, is a phenomenon that is difficult to understand, much less explain, given the lessons from our founding fathers, from economics and from history, as highlighted in the previous and following sections. Liberals clearly understand nothing about economics. Nor do they understand the flow of money and what creates wealth and what destroys it. A Liberal will vote every time for higher taxes on someone or something as long as that tax is not on them. But they are indeed clueless, because when you raise taxes on say a corporation, that corporation pays those taxes by increasing prices to consumers. Thus, the fool that votes for higher taxes, in the mistaken and ignorant belief that they will not impact him or her, always pays in the end. So, as taxes go up, the standard of living of Americans goes down, for almost everyone, but particularly for the poor and the middle class. As stated by Henry Hazlitt, "*The mounting burden of taxation not only undermines individual incentives to increased work and earnings, but in a score of ways discourages capital accumulation and distorts, unbalances, and shrinks production. Total real wealth and income are made smaller than it would otherwise be. On net balance there is more poverty rather than less.*"

As well, Liberals do not understand one of the most fundamental concepts of economics, and that is that "money follows productivity". The clearest way to illustrate this is, when you are working money flows to you because you are productive. But, when you stop working or retire, money flows away from you - to the producers of the goods and services that you still need to survive but are no longer working to produce. And Liberals do not understand that the government does not in and of itself produce anything, nor does it earn any money whatsoever, unless it sells public assets. So, the money collected by government through taxation, by taking from productive people and then spent by government, always flows away from non-productivity to companies or individuals who are productive. The only way that the money spent by government, or by extension by the people that the government gives that tax money to, is returned to government is through taxation; and the flight of capital from taxation to productivity starts all over again, being interrupted only by that long period of total non-productivity, which is when money is in the hands of government.

Also, what Liberals do not understand at all is, if you want less of something, you tax it and, if you want more of something, you subsidize it. Time and time again Liberals have increased taxes in one area, only to find that revenues decreased instead of increased, or that an activity that was subsidized actually created an unwanted abundance of that good or service through an unnatural distortion of the market. This is why Liberals simply do not understand that decreasing taxes actually produces more government revenues than does increasing taxes, which results in less government revenues. In fact, the sum total of all taxes – federal, state and local – has averaged about 30% of GDP throughout recent history, no matter what the tax rates are that have been imposed on the people. Liberals either do not understand this economic fact, or they will not admit to it, because if they did they would then have to confess to the American people that the current federal deficit cannot be solved by higher tax rates, because at the tax saturation level we are presently at, higher tax rates simply do not equate to higher tax revenues.

The economic theory that Liberals, and Obama in particular, subscribe to is called Keynesian Economics, after John Maynard Keynes. Keynes championed the theory that governments should spend money they do not have in difficult economic times to stimulate growth. This is in direct conflict with the economic theory to which Conservatives adhere to and that is supply side economics, where true productivity and job growth can only be attained by private industry and by private spending, which is best stimulated by low taxes and reasonable regulation. The Liberal economic theory of Keynesian economics has been proven time and time again to be not only unworkable but in fact damaging to the very economy that it is intended to help.

Some argue that Franklin Roosevelt's New Deal was the largest real-world test of the Keynesian Myth in recent history, and according even to FDR's Treasury Secretary Henry Morgenthau in sworn testimony before Congress on May 9, 1939, the New Deal was a failure; "*We have tried spending money. We are spending more than we have ever spent before and it does not work.*" And Morgenthau also told Congress: "*I say after eight years of this Administration we have just as much unemployment as when we started. ... And an enormous debt to boot!*

Keynesian economics has been equated to a large swimming pool, in which the water scooped from the deep end is added back to the shallow end in the hopes of making the shallow end of the pool deeper. Or, as stated by

Jonathon Moseley, Keynesian economics is, "… *the insane belief that the economy can be stimulated by government spending. It provides the excuse to depart from common sense that allows politicians to ignore the alarm bells. It is ludicrous mainly because our government doesn't have any money to spend*". No matter what the lessons of history have shown us with regards to economics, Liberals like Obama simply will not let go of the Keynesian Myth, that the government is the center of society, and as such that our entire economy depends on government spending. It should be noted, however, in all fairness to Keynes, that he believed governments should also save money in good times, so they could prop up their economies in bad times. However, Liberals only believe in half of Keynesian Theory - that of endless government spending and dept.

One of the most glaring examples of the cognitive dissonance of Liberal government spending, and the rhetoric associated with it, is what is called "baseline" budgeting, which is the method used by the federal government to calculate future budget requirements. As defined by Wikipedia, "*Baseline budgeting is an accounting method the United States federal government uses to develop a budget for future years. Baseline budgeting uses current spending levels as the "baseline" for establishing future funding requirements and assumes future budgets will equal the current budget times the inflation rate times the population growth rate…* [The baseline growth rate] i*s now approximately 6% increase per fiscal-year.*" What this means is that the federal government grows its budget by at least 6% a year, irrespective of economic conditions. And worse yet, any "decrease" to that projected growth rate is referred to by the CBO and by Democrats as a spending "cut". As a prime example of this craziness, the Republican budgets put forward in the last 10 years have included spending reductions – reductions for which the Republicans have been pilloried by the Left. Yet in all cases, the proposed Republican cuts actually were only reductions in the growth rate of government, for example from 6% to 2%, with no proposed cuts whatsoever to the previous year's budget. But, as a result of these Republican proposed budget growth moderations, the Democrats screamed that "Republicans want to kill your children and your grandparents" and of course the mindless Liberals and other low information voters bite on that rhetoric; hook, line and sinker, time and time again. In fact, just look at the screaming by Liberals during the current sequestration, in which only $85 B was cut from the 2013 federal budget, a paltry 2.2% of total expenditures.

With regards to real economics principles, why then are Liberals so compliant in being led down the wrong road by their own Party? They endlessly parrot their own Liberal talking points that "Wall Street greed" caused the housing crisis, without understanding that that the argument was a defensive one fabricated by Liberals in government to deflect the blame against who really caused the problem, and that was the Democrats who forced on the banks the concept of affordable housing for people who simply could not afford them. And Liberals somehow are secure in their belief that government policies cannot destroy entire economies. Yet, the one Liberal policy of "affordable housing" nearly took down the combined economies of the free world in 2008.

I ask, what is "Wall Street" and why do Liberals demonize that industry? People who work on Wall Street are simply middle men and women who facilitate the movement of money, whether it be to buy stocks, mutual funds and other investments for people, including government employees through their pension funds, and (or) to assist in the movement of capital from willing investors to entrepreneurs through the investment capital industry. People on Wall Street do not create regulation, they have no ability to impact you without your agreement to use their fees and services and they are normal professionals who provide much needed services for other people. Yet, somehow, according to Liberals and to Obama, the people who work on Wall Street instead of being respected must rather be vilified, hated and blamed for every mistake made by government – an disgrace that would not be possible without a compliant uneducated public that is not intelligent enough to understand reality from outright lies.

Liberals continue to support Unions that have turned from being important in the American workplace to now being institutions of greed and of the Left, destroying our nation's companies and its very life blood, including the ability to manufacture at a profit, to produce, to be energy independent and to keep our money and thus our standard of living in this country, rather than to export permanently it to the Middle East and to China. Why can't anyone on the Left see this? It is as obvious as knowing it is you when you look in the mirror!

Liberals do not believe in the free enterprise system and they believe that large corporations are bad because they make a profit. But we Conservatives ask, what is a large company, as compared to a small company? A large company is simply a large group of individuals that make products or performs services for individuals and society that a small company or small group cannot. For example, a small company cannot produce cars or airplanes. Only large groups of talented individuals working together can do that. And who actually owns these large companies? A majority of the large corporations in America are public companies that are owned by their shareholders. And, a majority of those shareholders are either government or private pension funds or individual investors, like mom or dad, or grandma and grandpa, who are trying to get some return on their investment savings so that they can retire comfortably. And, if a large company is successful, it is successful only because other people desire its goods or services and need or want them and, as a result, purchase them. While Liberals like Obama hate "big pharmaceutical" companies, amongst many others, where would the health of this nation be without all of the wonder drugs created by billions in high risk R&D spending by these companies? This example can be extended to all companies in America and across the world, especially to the healthcare and health insurance agencies, which the Left loves to excoriate daily. For you on the Left who mimic the Liberal talking points about "obscene profits" in the healthcare industry, according to a 2008 CNN review, the health insurance industry ranks 22nd in profits out of 53 sectors, making a 4.6% profit as a percentage of revenues. This is while the remaining healthcare sectors ranked from 30th to 39th, making just 3.0% to 1.3% profits, respectively. Obscene profits - really?

To expand on the Liberal and Obama foolishness of loathing the fact that successful companies make a profit, let's look at real world economics. In the present day stock market, the average valuation of DOW listed companies is a PE ratio that is about 14 times earnings. This means that the price of the stock is valued at a ratio of 14 times that company's current annual earnings per share. This average positive market valuation of a multiple to current earnings is because these companies are deemed by the market to have excellent growth potential for the future. However, in a Utopian Obama world, companies would not make a profit at all, because all excess earnings would be confiscated and redistributed by Obama and by government. But, if a company did not make a profit, it could not grow, nor could it innovate, because growth and innovation require that capital be tied up in R&D and in debt for that company to expand. Why is this? This is because, R&D expenditures require that large amounts of capital be consumed by non-producing activities for long periods of time, so excess capital (from profits) must be available to invest in R&D and in growth. So, no growth, no innovation and as a result the valuation of that company in the market would be 1 times earnings, at best. If that were the case, the current stock market would be valued at ~1,100 on the Dow, instead of the current ~15,000, and companies simply would not grow. As a result, most of our nation's companies would not exist at all and no new products would be produced.

Obama and the Left think that corporate profits only go to certain select rich individuals, but there is nothing further from the truth. *All* of the profits from major companies are spent at some point on innovation and growth, or they are returned to their shareholders via dividends. And, in America these companies must show a profit in spite of massive new regulations increasingly imposed by Obama and the Left, and they must show a profit in spite of America having the highest taxes on corporate profits in the world.

So, where would this country be without large and small businesses? We would be living in caves or small dwellings, freezing and trying to live off the land, with none of the amenities available to us that we presently enjoy in modern society. And more importantly, most of us would not be here at all, because subsistence level agrarianism cannot produce enough food for large populations. As highlighted above, the profits earned by large and small business are what create jobs, allow for capital investment in new products and services and provide for the innovation necessary to improve the standard of living of all Americans and many others around the world. To attack business in America, or anywhere else, either through class warfare or through punitive taxes and regulations, is simply to attack the very foundation of our standard of living and our way of life. And, Obama and the Left forget another major thing, without companies, without innovation and profit and without a successful free enterprise system there would be no money at all for their dearly beloved government.

Liberals also love to attack the "rich", promoting even further their brand of class envy, divisiveness and hatred. But, like the old saying goes, "*Have you ever been given a job by a poor person*?" What would the impact be on this country and others if a percentage of the population was not "rich"? Well for one thing we would not have the tax income we have, because the top 1% of income earners pays 37% of the taxes. Also, if everyone had the same income level, as desired by Liberals, wouldn't it really mean that there would be no excellence in our society at all? This is because people who make large sums of money do so because they developed an idea that is useful to society (e.g. Bill Gates, computer operating system), or they are part of a larger group/company that produces products desired by people (e.g., IPhones), or are they particularly talented such that many people are willing to pay to see them perform (e.g., sports figures, Oprah, Hollywood actors), to name a few. Conversely, if the entire wealth of the rich was simply confiscated by the government, as Obama wishes to do, there would be no incentive for anyone to excel in the quality of their efforts and ideas, and all of us in society would suffer accordingly.

The US federal debt is now at $16.4 T and is rising by about 100 billion a month. And, it has increased by $5.9 T during Obama's four years in office. Worse yet, combined state debt totals a further $4 T for a government debt total that is over $20 T, not counting a further $ 1 T in student loan debt and $11.2 T in household debt. Yet Liberals like Obama, say "No" to any sort of spending cuts and only want to raise taxes further. Yet Obama's proposed higher taxes for people making more than $250 K, because it is "fair", would have only funded government for about 8 days a year, as estimated by the CBO. It is also estimated by the CBO that future unfunded liabilities for federal government entitlement programs, such as Social Security, Medicare and Medicaid are estimated to be at least $144 T over the next 30 years, or approximately $2 M per taxpayer. With the total net value of all holdings in the US estimated to be about $60 T, this means that the federal government has agreed to spending for social programs that is at least three times the net worth of the entire country, including the underwater promises by state governments! To further highlight the problems we face, just to service the current federal debt, when interest rates return to their historical average of 5.4%, the payment on the debt will increase from $360 billion today to $1 T. This is beyond insanity, yet Liberals scream at the very concept of reduced spending, saying that Republicans want to "kill our children" and "throw granny out into the street".

What has happened to this great country? These tax and spend supporters are mindless automatons who are killing all of our futures. And, wait until draconian cuts in government spending are required, and those cuts will be required soon and they will need to be across the board, because the current rate of spending is unsustainable. When these cuts happen, the Liberals in America, like those in Greece and elsewhere, will riot in the streets, demanding their government checks, creating civil disorder and acting lawlessly, as they have already done at the anti-Wall Street "Occupy" rallies. And, worse yet, they reelect for president the moron who, we Conservatives believe, is intentionally bankrupting this country.

Us Conservatives have tried to educate our Liberal friends and family about the dangers ahead from the bloated government debt, but they refuse to listen, even to the extent of putting their hands to their ears and shouting "blah, blah" blah" like spoiled rotten children. Or they call us racist or any other name they can think of. The debt is a result of true greed at the highest level, and it spells the destruction of America, and soon. The end result will be a much lower standard of living for all Americans, but those who will be hurt the most will be the poor and middle class - the very people who are supporting these insane policies. And, these people should be completely ashamed of themselves and of their greed, but rather they attack the messenger of the obvious and the inevitable.

Liberals are in fact taking money from their own children and grandchildren. What could be worse, and what kind of a person would do that? But we know what kind of person it is – it is a mindless American Liberal who thinks this way, while at the same time deriding Conservatives and the Republican Party for attempting to be fiscally responsible. And, while all this is occurring, Liberals keep insisting that they are the morally superior political party. This has to become the new definition of maximum insanity – a cognitive dissonance of breathtaking proportions.

The reality is, with all the endless and numerous taxes we already have in this country on almost every activity, the federal government will collect only about $2.7 T in taxes this year. Yet it will spend at least $3.8 T. In 1970, the entire federal budget was $195 B. Thus, government spending today represents an insane increase of 1,844% over 1970 spending levels. Yet, the Liberals scream that we are not spending enough. There are no words in the English language to describe this type of senseless thinking!

One of the better quotes regarding the Liberal concept of government and economics is from Ronald Reagan, who stated, "*Government's view of the economy could be summed up in a few short phrases: If it moves, tax it. If it keeps moving, regulate it. And if it stops moving, subsidize it*". As well, Reagan said, "*No government ever voluntarily reduces itself in size. Government programs, once launched, never disappear. Actually, a government bureau is the nearest thing to eternal life we'll ever see on this earth*!"

Right now the US federal government debt totals $52,267 for every man, women and child in the US, or $143,849 per household. Of that, in four years Obama has increased the debt by about $18,692 for every man, women and child in the US, or about $51,444 per US household. **Obama's debt now totals more than the entire debt accumulated by all 41 US presidents from George Washington to Bill Clinton**. And remember that Obama called George W. Bush's debt of $2 T over eight years "immoral". Worse yet, Liberals in America recently were dumb enough to vote for Obama a second time, believing that he is the best person to handle the economy. To us Conservatives, this is incredulous!

And, for those Liberals who want to believe that the government can continue down the current debt path with no impact to you, and that all you have to do to fix the problem is to raise taxes on the rich and that Obama would never abandon you in his promise to only raise taxes on the upper 2% of wage earners, this is absolutely not the case as quoted from Mail Online a British website on January 4, 2013, "*Middle-class workers will take a bigger hit to their income proportionately than those earning between $200,000 and $500,000 under the new fiscal cliff deal, according to the nonpartisan Tax Policy Center. Earners in the latter group will pay an average 1.3 percent more - or an additional $2,711 - in taxes this year, while workers making between $30,000 and $200,000 will see their paychecks shrink by as much as 1.7 percent - or up to $1,784 - the D.C.-based think tank reported. Overall, nearly 80 percent of households will pay more money to the federal government as a result of the fiscal cliff deal.*"

So Liberals, Obama lied to you, your taxes have already gone up, but even worse, this is not going to reduce the deficit as also promised by Obama. Government spending as part of the fiscal cliff deal is going increase by $4 T over the next 10 years. And further, even after the fiscal cliff deal, Obama wants to raise taxes yet again. So, because of the Liberal voter, we continue this never ending cycle of insanity – the government increases taxes to "pay" for increased spending, but instead the government increases spending, then it increases taxes again to "pay" for that increased spending, but it continues to spend, followed by more taxes, followed by more spending, followed by higher taxes, followed by even higher spending….and at some point taxes have to go up punitively on *all* Americans, as they are now. And wait until the government wants to confiscate your savings and your retirement plan, which has already happened in Cyprus and is something Obama actually has proposed.

For the record, Conservative economists such as Milton Friedman warned 14 years ago when it began that the Liberal utopian socioeconomic experiment of a single currency for Europe, the Euro, would fail, based on fundamental economic principles. However, Obama still wants to follow a Euro-socialist model, in spite of the fact that the entire Euro zone is collapsing presently, as predicted by Friedman, with tremendously negative consequences to the people involved, including 50% unemployment in Greece. In fact the Former German Finance Minister Oskar Lafontaine, who is known as the architect of the euro, even referred to his own brainchild recently as a "catastrophe". "*The economic situation is worsening from month to month*," he wrote on his Left party blog. "*Unemployment has reached a level that puts democratic structures ever more in doubt.*"

Most Liberals do not understand this, but even now government is growing through Obama's and Bernanke's policies at the expense of the people. This is because most of us "normal" folks scrimp and save money over our working careers in the hope of retiring comfortably. But even so, we need to grow our money through investments to have any chance at all of having a comfortable retirement. But, the federal government is consuming all of the excess money in our economy presently and it is intentionally keeping interest rates exceedingly low to keep interest on the government debt within manageable limits. This means that people who save for retirement can get virtually no return on their investments. For many this means that their investments have either not grown or have shrunk over the last five years – a huge impact on the "middle class" that has tremendous negative long term consequences and which no one talks about.

Regarding the US economy, and where it is headed in terms of government spending and Liberal greed, Alexander Fraser Tytler was credited as saying, "*A democracy cannot exist as a permanent form of government. It can only exist until the voters discover that they can vote themselves largesse from the public treasury. From that moment on, the majority always votes for the candidates promising the most benefits from the public treasury with the result that a democracy always collapses over loose fiscal policy, always followed by a dictatorship. The average age of the world's greatest civilizations has been about 200 years. These nations have progressed through this sequence: 'From bondage to spiritual faith; From spiritual faith to great courage; From courage to liberty; From liberty to abundance; From abundance to selfishness; From selfishness to apathy; From apathy to dependence; From dependence back into bondage*". Unfortunately, we Conservatives fear that the country is near the very end of this progression.

32 THE FREE ENTERPRISE SYSTEM – WHY IS IT THE FAIREST?

Conservatives believe that the free enterprise system, coupled with limited government interference, is not only the best and the fairest economic system for America, but it is also the best and the fairest system for the rest of the world. But, why do Conservatives both believe and stand by this, while Liberals in America champion the opposite - that the best economic system is socialism enforced by a far-reaching federal government that supports the redistribution of wealth and statism?

First and foremost, free markets and capitalism are based on the concepts of liberty, self-determination and entrepreneurship, with rewards determined by unbiased market forces. In other words, these market forces have no politics, they see no color or social status and they are undeniably both completely impartial and fair because they allow any individual or group of individuals the maximum potential for economic mobility and achievement, if they work hard, take risks and succeed. These market forces work for the good because they benefit society in every way. After all, to be successful in a free market system, an individual or group of individuals (companies) prospers only when they produce goods and services that other people want and are able to purchase, meaning that the producers and the consumers are both benefited at the same time. And, each and every transaction consists of a willing seller and a willing buyer and thus is mutually agreed upon. As a result, free markets produce the greatest rewards for societies, and these rewards are among the reasons that America is the greatest and most prosperous nation on earth, at least for now, and it is the reason that other countries should also embrace free market concepts and have been doing so more and more.

Success in a free market capitalist system requires both hard work and a willingness to take risks, requirements that Obama and Liberals simply do not understand, because all they want to do is to add more and more risk to the people through punitive regulation and taxation. They also do not understand that an economy is simply the sum of all economic transactions that occur during any given period, and as such each and every person in society is part of that economy, such that punitive government interference on any part of an economy affects the entire system. And, especially for small businesses, which create 70% of the jobs in America, the risks today are significant, because they include the potential loss of everything a person has ever worked for, if their business fails as a result of punitive government intervention.

In a free market system, all of the needs and wants of the people are met, and they are met efficiently. This is because the free enterprise system within modern society comprises millions of individuals, all of whom are constantly looking for niches in which they can innovate and prosper. Consequently, new products and services are created and brought to market both cost efficiently and quickly. This efficient and people friendly system, supported by free association, is in direct contrast to the inefficiencies, shortages and limited consumer choices that are characteristic of economies "planned" by centralized governments and run by socialist "nirvanists". The billions and billions of daily transactions that make up a modern economy, and the millions and millions of ideas that are being fostered and considered every day to improve and innovate the economy, simply cannot be replaced by any form of central or even decentralized government planning – but Liberals simply will never understand this.

I have had Liberals from other countries, especially from Latin America, tell me that "*Socialism is the best economic system for poor people because it is the only system that gives them true upward economic mobility.*" But, this is pure bunk. In a free market capitalist society, a man or a woman can have an idea, and by working hard to promote that idea become prosperous, or even exceedingly wealthy. In fact, this phenomenon has been referred to in America for 233 years as the "American Dream". And, America is not only replete with millions of individual economic success stories, these stories from the sum of all of these great people and their economic successes, whether small or large, provide the foundation for the prosperity and triumph of our entire nation. Conversely, the Marxist model of forced wealth redistribution and forced government involvement neither creates wealth nor does it create true happiness - rather it fosters servitude, malaise and indolence. Nations, and by extension their populaces, do not become wealthy and grow as a result of redistributing wealth - it first takes free enterprise and entrepreneurship to create that wealth to begin with, the wealth that the Marxists latter confiscate to redistribute.

Henry Hazlitt, a distinguished economist, noted, "*The way to get a maximum rate of "economic growth"...is to give maximum encouragement to production, employment, saving, and investment. And the way to do this is to maintain a free market and a sound currency. It is to encourage profits, which must in turn encourage both investment and employment. It is to refrain from oppressive taxation that siphons away the funds that would otherwise be available for investment. It is to allow free wage rates that permit and encourage full employment. It is to allow free interest rates, which would tend to maximize saving and investment.*

The way to slow down the rate of economic growth is, of course, precisely the opposite of this. It is to discourage production, employment, saving, and investment by incessant interventions, controls, threats, and harassment. It is to frown upon profits, to declare that they are excessive, to file constant antitrust suits, to control prices by law or by threats, to levy confiscatory taxes that discourage new investment and siphon off the funds that make investment possible, to hold down interest rates artificially to the point where real saving is discouraged and malinvestment encouraged, to deprive employers of genuine freedom of bargaining, to grant excessive immunities and privileges to labor unions so that their demands are chronically excessive and chronically threaten unemployment--and then to try to offset all these policies by government spending, deficits, and monetary inflation...

[Statists'] recipe for inducing growth always turns out to be--inflation. This does lead to the illusion of growth, which is measured in their statistics in monetary terms. [But]...the magic of inflation is always a short-run magic, and quickly played out...The consequences of this short-lived paradise are malinvestment, waste, a wanton redistribution of wealth and income, the growth of speculation and gambling, immorality and corruption, social resentment, discontent and upheaval, disillusion, bankruptcy, increased governmental controls, and eventual collapse. This year's euphoria becomes next year's hangover. Sound long-run growth is always retarded."

In American, we are truly in an epic battle between free market capitalism and socialism - between god an evil, between individualism and collectivism and between liberty and servitude. As Mr. Hazlitt wrote, to attack the free enterprise system, as Obama and the Liberals have been doing more and more recently, is to attack "*economic freedom--which means, in fact, the whole of human freedom.*" I agree with Mr. Hazlitt that what is threatened by the statists, the Marxists, the centralized planners, the socialists, the Liberals and by Obama "*is no less than our present civilization itself.*" And, the earlier question of why do Liberals support socialism over free market capitalism must incontrovertibly be met with the answer, "*Since it makes no sense to support socialism economically, it must be that Liberals support socialism because it allows maximum control and power over the people.*"

33 SOCIALIZED MEDICINE

In perhaps the most glaring example of legislative activism, against the wishes of approximately 67 percent of the American people at the time, a slim 51 person majority of Democrats in the Senate in 2010 pushed through the socialized healthcare plan now referred to as Obamacare. The Bill was never approved by the House, nor did it get the 60 votes required for passage in the Senate. Rather it was passed by a process never used before for a new bill and that was by "reconciliation". To illustrate the level of outright abuse that was employed to pass this bill using the reconciliation process, the following is quoted from About.com:

> "*This federal budget reconciliation process arose from language inserted in the Congressional Budget and Impoundment Control Act of 1974, which, in part, allows Senators to pass concurrent budget bills without debate or a presidential signature. Following passage of the 1974 Act, several senators attempted to attach amendments which had nothing to do with fiscal policy to reconciliation bills. To ensure important legislative initiatives are given proper checks and balances, subsequent reconciliation bills have adopted the "Byrd Rule," which applies to amendments that:*
>
> - *Do not produce a change in outlays or revenues.*
> - *Produce changes in outlays or revenue which are merely incidental to the non-budgetary components of the provision.*
> - *Are outside the jurisdiction of the committee that submitted the title or provision for inclusion in the reconciliation measure.*
> - *Increase outlays or decrease revenue if the provision's title, as a whole, fails to achieve the Senate reporting committee's reconciliation instructions.*
> - *Increase net outlays or decrease revenue during a fiscal year after the years covered by the reconciliation bill unless the provision's title, as a whole, remains budget neutral.*
> - *Contain recommendations regarding the OASDI (social security) trust funds*".

Clearly, none of the above applies to Obamacare – it was simply not a budget bill – and as such it is true that Harry Reid passed the bill illegally, although with the Democrats controlling the Senate nothing can now be done about it.

To understand very simply the irrationality of desiring a government funded single payer system, which Obama himself states that Obamacare is simply the first step towards, we need to be aware of the following statistics. In 2012 the US spent an estimated 17.9% of GDP on healthcare. With a national GDP of $15.1 T, that means that $2.7 T was spent on healthcare in the US or $8,593 per person. The total revenue from all federal tax receipts in 2012 was $2.5 T. That means that if the federal government paid for healthcare in entirety under the Left's desired single payer system – a system called "free" healthcare by the Left – the entire annual revenue of the federal government would not have funded all of the healthcare expenditures incurred in that year, never mind the need for funding the rest of the federal government, including the military, education, Social Security, etc.

Due to the new costs associated with Obamacare, healthcare expenditures in 2013 are expected to rise 7.9%, to $2.91 T or to $9,272 per person. That translates to $25,519 per year per household. However, because 47% of people in the US pay no federal income tax whatsoever, and thus these people would not pay for healthcare under a federal single payer system, the total becomes $48,149 per year for the 53% of households that actually pay an income tax. So, for you Liberals who have been voting for Democrats and for Obama because you want your "free" healthcare, and especially for those who are in higher income brackets, the numbers presented herein are real and unassailable. You know the saying, "*If you think healthcare is expensive now, wait until it is free.*"

So, how can we explain that Obamacare was only going to cost $848 M over 10 years, according to Harry Reid in 2010? This is because it is only a partial step toward a single payer system and more importantly that the bill is so complicated no one understood it then or even understands it now. In fact, soon after its passage Max Baucus the Democrat Senator from Montana conceded that the cost of Obamacare would be at least $2.6 T over 10 years, excluding the estimated cost of the doc fix, which would add a further $300 B, bringing the total closer to $3.0 T. And, as well, the closer the program gets to implementation in 2014, the higher the costs are projected to be, as estimated by the CBO.

What Liberals refuse to comprehend is that the least efficient way to run any program is to have the federal government do it, and it is especially frightening that so many people are willing to put their very health in the hands of the federal government. Even John Maynard Keynes wrote, "*Government machinery has been described as a marvelous labor saving device which enables ten men to do the work of one*".

Of greater relevance is to look at the countries in which socialized medicine is being practiced today. *A recent study by David Green and Laura Casper, "Delay, Denial and Dilution," written for the London-based Institute of Economic Affairs, concludes that the British healthcare services are just about the worst in the developed world"*. And those writers also state, "*Do we need to experience this for the next 30-40 years before we draw the same conclusions*?

Further, in countries with socialized medicine, patients can wait up to nine months for an MRI and the death rates for almost all forms of cancer are much higher than they are in the US. This is because all forms of socialized medicine must eventually employ rationing of services. Not only does the quality of healthcare go down measurably in a socialized system, due in part to low doctor pay and the need to use poorly skilled foreign doctors and to a lessor availability of high-tech equipment, but older people are often denied care and die earlier than they normally would have because of their age. Professor Patrick Pullicino of Great Britain recently wrote that, "*NHS doctors are prematurely ending the lives of thousands of elderly hospital patients because they are difficult to manage or to free up beds… The NHS kills off up to 120,000 patients a year*". As well, a recent article (July 13, 2013) by the medical director of the British National Health System (NHS) concluded "*that in just 14 trusts in England have been responsible for up to 13,000 "excess deaths" since 2005*". These were not just old people that were forced to die early, these numbers include young and middle age people that died as a result of neglect, including "*alarming levels of infections, patients suffering from neglect and appalling blunders such as surgery performed on the wrong parts of bodies*". Yet, Obama still constantly refers to Britain's NHS as an exemplary example of the "success" of socialized medicine.

Terrifyingly, the implementation of Obamacare will require as estimated 25,000 pages of new laws and the program will be administered by the IRS, an out of control punitive organization that Americans cannot now trust due to the recent scandal regarding the targeting of Conservative groups, which translates to outright voter suppression and indisputably to government tyranny and the abuse of the people's 1st Amendment rights. Worse yet, as part of the Obamacare act, in 2015 Obama will appoint 15 people to a Board that will oversee all aspects of Obamacare, including deciding who gets coverage and treatment and who gets it for what. The way this Board is structured is that it will not need congressional approval, it will not be subject to congressional oversight and nor will it be subject to even a presidential veto. Citizens will have NO authority to challenge the Board's pronouncements in court, and thus for the first time America will have a group of political appointees that will not be answerable to the people, even for something as important as their very lives.

America presently has the best healthcare system in the world, but Liberals probably have already destroyed it, like they have destroyed or will destroy everything else. In order to improve our healthcare system further, Conservatives had proposed allowing insurance pools that can be purchased across state lines, permitting people to set up tax free medical savings accounts (MSA's) and substantial reforms of the federal government Medicare and Medicaid programs. But instead, the Liberal worships at the altar of "free" healthcare and believes somehow that healthcare is his or her "right", even though what they actually mean by that right is that someone else should have to pay for it, because Liberals also believe that they should not have to provide for either themselves or for their family.

Well, now that Liberals have what they want with the unconscionable Obamacare law, we will just have to wait and see how well everyone in the nation really likes it, especially when the average person's cost for healthcare doubles, when the care standard becomes much lower overall and when the likelihood happens that you may die before your time when you are denied a lifesaving treatment because you are too old, or worse yet because you are a Conservative and disagree with the government. And young folks who support this Obamanation do not realize that this healthcare law is actually the greatest transfer of wealth from the young to old in history.

Although we may indeed have to wait at see the full impact of Obamacare - not for implementation of the law for individuals, which goes into effect in 2014 - but now we may have to wait until 2015 for full implementation of the law for businesses, according to Obama's recent statements in which he states that he (illegally so) wants to put off that portion of the law to 2015, noticeably to after the mid-term elections. We should all ask, if this law is so great, why put it off? We all know the answer to that question.

34 WELFARE & ENTITLEMENTS

Liberals demonize Conservatives every day about welfare and entitlements, calling Conservatives selfish, racist or worse. But a Liberal is never willing to look at actual statistics and facts regarding the hugely negative impacts that welfare and entitlements have on individuals and on society. For all people on welfare, but especially for Black people in America, I refer to the Democrat Party's support of generational welfare as "socioeconomic slavery". Rather than believing what we Conservatives believe, that the sky is the limit for every person in society, no matter their color, creed or socioeconomic status, Liberals have been enslaving Black people in America for generations with their welfare policies. Why all people cannot see this truth as self-evident remains to us Conservatives as one of the greatest mysteries of all time.

It has been shown, and it is easy to research should any Liberal want to do so, that in the early 1960's Black people in America had a higher overall marriage percentage rate than did whites. Today, in a socially catastrophic turnaround, approximately 76% of Black children are born out of wedlock – sentencing the "family" and the young people involved to a life of higher crime, poverty, lower education and a lower overall standard of living. While there is not one person in this country who does not have compassion regarding these statistics, or should have, no one wants to look at the root causes. While we Conservatives strongly believe that generation welfare is cruel - that it destroys people, families and entire generations - the Liberal mindset is such that, if a Conservative opposes this form of government oppression, they are called racist, insensitive, selfish or worse.

Numerous very illustrative studies have been conducted on the impact of welfare by researchers both black and white. These studies have shown definitively that the negative impact to Black families is entirely due to Liberal government policies – which are composed of rules regarding the receipt of welfare that are directly contrary to marriage. For example, if both persons of a couple are on welfare they lose those government benefits if they marry, thus ensuring that marriage is not an option. All of society is to blame for the low Black marriage rate. But, while many want to blame this on the decline of Black culture, it is really Liberal policies that that have created these problems for lower income Black families in America.

Worse yet, welfare laws in the US are set up to reward a single mother who gives birth to numerous children with government benefits of up to $2,500 per child per month, or more. It has been reported recently that a single mother in the US can receive benefits from the federal government totaling as much as $55,000 per year, and that a single mother with four kids can increase that "take" by ~50%. No wonder those people vote for Democrats, irrespective of the impact these Liberal policies have on the public debt and on society. Sadly, the recipients themselves do not understand that they have been forced into a form of socioeconomic slavery – not that they have to work for these benefits as a slave would – but that they are imprisoned into a socioeconomic position where they have no incentive or opportunity to improve either themselves or the lives of their children. And worse yet, these policies support record numbers of single parents, with the attendant problems of higher poverty, lower education and income levels and greater incarceration rates.

When I see the housing "Projects" of New Orleans, Texas and the South, I am deeply saddened by what we have done to people as a society, but even more so what Liberal policies have done to our fellow Americans. That Black people in America do not understand their plight and predicament, nor the root cause of it, is perhaps even sadder yet. At the same time, when a Conservative suggests that the Liberal policies that enslave people ought to be changed, we are vilified in the most heinous terms by the Liberals, who are in fact the direct cause of this suffering in America.

No one in America should be allowed to live on generational welfare and no one should collect public benefits for more than a very short period, say one year, unless they are truly disabled. But, we presently have entire groups of lawyers in the US that for a fee get perfectly able bodied Americans signed on to permanent government disability benefits. This reference, written by Mark Krikorian on July 26, 2012, highlights how far this country has strayed from reality under the Liberal, socialistic state, "*Today is the 22nd anniversary of the Americans with Disabilities Act, and the Census Bureau proudly notes that nearly 1 in 5 Americans is now disabled. Or, rather, "disabled". A new report from the bureau notes the various types of disabilities, some of which are inarguable: deafness, blindness, Alzheimer's, autism. But there are others that might strike the reader as more dubious: "Had difficulty with schoolwork," "Was limited in the kind or amount of housework," "Had difficulty finding a job or remaining employed," and "Had difficulty getting along with other children of the same age." The report notes that from 2005 to 2010, the number of "disabled" people grew by 2.2 million, to 56.7 million. Also, "In 2008, the federal government spent* *an estimated $357 billion dollars on programs for working-age people with disabilities, representing 12 percent of total federal outlays.*" This is yet another example of the continuing legacy of Liberal insanity – insanity in this case that has a tremendous negative impact on individuals, on families and on children on a generational basis.

I ask you Liberals, who is at fault for the fact that, "*Statistics from the Department of Justice indicate that Black males are incarcerated – held in prison or jail – at a rate that is over 6 times higher than that for white males?*" We Conservatives believe that you Liberals are directly responsible for these statistics, because these facts are a direct result of the socioeconomic slavery you invented and continue to support, and for which you ought to be supremely ashamed of.

With regards to ongoing Liberal arguments that only government can take care of the poor, Tom Trinko recently wrote for the American Thinker, "*The liberal position is that the poor are too incompetent or stupid to actually take care of themselves. Of course the liberals don't use the pejoratives out loud, but liberals do declare that the poor can't take care of themselves without the aid of liberal politicians funneling other people's money to them. Given that minorities make up a disproportionately large fraction of the poor in America it's incredibly racist for liberals to declare that the poor are incapable of taking care of themselves. But then liberals, like their KKK founding forefathers, have always believed that Blacks are incapable of taking care of themselves and need caring compassionate white folk, i.e. liberals, to watch over them.*"

To further refute the lie that only Liberals care about the poor, Conservatives believe that we as a country should help provide less fortunate people in this nation with a hand up (i.e., Ronald Reagan's safety net), but that ongoing and permanent handouts destroy the very futures that we as a society are trying to improve. With regards to the impacts of welfare irrespective of race, in a 1996 article by Patrick F. Fagan, Ph.D. and Robert Rector, the authors concluded the following:

> "*It is welfare dependence, not poverty that has the most negative effect on children. Recent research by Congressional Budget Office Director June O'Neill shows that increasing the length of time a child spends on welfare may reduce the child's IQ by as much as 20 percent.*
>
> *Welfare dependency as a child has a negative effect on the earnings and employment capacity of young men. The more welfare income received by a boy's family during his childhood, the lower the boy's earnings will be as an adult, even when compared to boys in*

families with identical non-welfare income.

Welfare also plays a powerful role in promoting illegitimacy. Research by CBO Director O'Neill also shows, for example, that a 50 percent increase in monthly AFDC and food stamp benefit levels will cause a 43 percent increase in the number of illegitimate births within a state. Illegitimacy, in turn, has an enormous negative effect on children's development and on their behavior as adults. Being born outside of marriage and raised in single parent homes:

- *Triples the level of behavioral and emotional problems among children;*
- *Nearly triples the level of teen sexual activity;*
- *Doubles the probability a young woman will have children out of wedlock; and,*
- *Doubles the probability a boy will become a threat to society, engage in criminal activity, and wind up in jail.*

Overall, welfare operates as a form of social toxin. The more of this toxin received by a child's family, the less successful the child will be as an adult. If America's children are to be saved, the current welfare system must be replaced. The automatic and rapid growth of welfare spending must be curtailed. Welfare should no longer be a one-way handout; recipients should be required to work for benefits received. Steps must be taken to reduce future illegitimacy, beginning with restricting cash welfare to unmarried teen mothers."

In spite of the statistics quoted above regarding the negative impacts of welfare, while Bill Clinton imposed a requirement to work for people receiving welfare benefits as part of his welfare reform package in an attempt to reduce welfare spending and servitude nationwide, Obama has done the exact opposite recently. It was reported on July 13, 2012 that, "*Yesterday the Obama administration gutted those federal work rules, ignoring the will of Congress by issuing a policy directive that allows the Department of Health and Human Services to waive the work requirements for the Temporary Assistance for Needy Families (TANF) program. "The result is the end of welfare reform," wrote Robert Rector and Kiki Bradley of The Heritage Foundation.*" While the Obama administration unilaterally granted itself this waiver authority, one that actually does not exist in any approved legislation, the administration is now saying it won't actually use this waiver to weaken work requirements. But, who we ask would believe anything Obama says – if you aren't going to use it why issue the directive? We need to get people off of welfare, but Obama is doing the exact opposite and he is enslaving them.

35 THE PHENOMENON OF CALIFORNIA

Because I live in Nevada, next to the state of California, I have watched the people of California, as well as individuals in my own family, continue down the road of "vote for a Democrat no matter the end result". These people somehow think that they are sophisticated and smart. In fact, they think they are smarter and more sophisticated than anyone else in the country, but the reality is that they have destroyed what once was a great state by continuing to vote for Liberal policies. Only about 15 years ago, California had the fifth largest economy in the world, but it has now dropped to the eighth largest economy. And, it is for the first time suffering population decline, as people exit the state for better conditions. The reason for this is that the people of California have been voting for Democrats for years, no matter the quality or the impact, and seem conditioned to do so, as rats are conditioned to run a maze. On the average, the state of California adopts about 800 new laws a year (to wit; 860 new California laws were adopted as of January 1, 2013). As well, spending by state government is so out of control that only California and Illinois (Obamas home state) have the lowest credit ratings of any state in the union. Not only are taxes obscenely high in California, but the thousands of laws adopted by the Democrat-controlled legislatures have made it illegal to do almost everything – extending almost to life itself.

Yet, the disease of Liberalism is so firmly ensconced in California that the people have become mere automatons, voting year in and year out for their accelerating loss of freedom, higher taxes and an encroaching lower standard of living. Recently, it was announced that for the first time in four years, the unemployment rate in California fell below 10%, as compared to 7.6% nationwide. Yet, no Republican presidential candidate even visits the state anymore.

To further illustrate the Liberal mindset in California, several Left wing extremist Democrat state congressmen recently began the process of introducing numerous (10) anti fracking bills, which almost assuredly will pass in the Liberal controlled state House and Senate in some form or another. This is in spite of the fact that arguably California is on the verge of a new black gold rush, with estimates that 15 billion barrels of oil could be accessed from the Monterey Shale formation by using hydraulic fracturing, or fracking. This safe method of recovering oil would result in millions of high paying jobs, lower energy costs and perhaps billions of dollars of tax revenues to the state, yet the California Liberals oppose what would be good for the people and for the state.

No matter that Liberal policies, regulation and spending have in essence destroyed what was once arguably our greatest state, the people in California are so acculturated into mindless Liberal ideology that they actually voted in 2012 to again raise taxes on higher income earners, which will further accelerate the downward spiral. We Conservatives observe and say, "spending in California is out of control", but the automatons in the state only respond by selecting "Yes" on the "raise taxes" portion of the ballot. California is a prime example of the problems facing this great nation. Look at this state closely and be forewarned. High rates of government spending, whether they are at the state or federal level, do not ensure prosperity. Rather, they guarantee the opposite - a state in decline hurrying over the cliff, as extreme far left-wing ideologues like Nancy Pelosi and Dianne Feinstein unfathomably get elected time and time again.

36 OBAMA

I have said previously that it is my personal opinion that, given time, Obama will be recognized without a doubt as the worst president every elected in the history of America, now or in the future, and eventually it will be known that it was Obama who destroyed America. However, I do believe now that, especially with the recent scandals of the Obama administration, some people are finally beginning to realize what an abysmal president this man is. But of course most Liberals will never admit to this.

Simply put, Obama is a far left wing, socialist ideologue who is against everything that is great about America. But, worse yet, he is for the entire list of what one would do if you really wanted to destroy this country. The man is arrogant and he is a narcissist and a sociopathic liar. And, with quotes from his book such as "*White folk's greed runs a world in need*", he is clearly a racist as well. And most importantly, he does not understand what he was elected and sworn to defend, and that is the Constitution of the United States. This was especially evident when he said, "*The Supreme Court never ventured into the issues of redistribution of wealth and sort of basic issues of political and economic justice in this society, and to that extent as radical as people try to characterize the Warren Court, it wasn't that radical… It didn't break free from the essential constraints that were placed by the founding fathers in the Constitution, at least as it has been interpreted. And the Warren court interpreted it generally in the same way -- that the Constitution is a document of negative liberties, says what the states can't do to you, says what the federal government can't do to you, but it doesn't say what the federal government or the state government must do on your behalf, and that hasn't shifted*". To this I say, "Mr. Obama, there are 17 enumerated powers that say exactly what the federal government must do on the behalf of the people – can't you read?"

In the Preamble to this book, I remark that, "*These Liberal activists instead went into politics or into the universities, where they could be removed from reality. And they became the people who would take our 1960's and 1970's radicalism and turn it into a political platform, and then use it some 40 years later to destroy not only America and our own futures, but also our children's futures and the very foundations of our society.*" The worst of these 1960's Liberal activists is of course Obama, who is a self-admitted extreme Left wing radical and whose ideology has become even more radicalized since that time.

Obama's class warfare and constant attempts to split America into groups, either to be supported or denigrated, are dividing this country and are destroying the social fabric of our nation. That, combined with his almost senseless support of irresponsible debt spending and his outright unwillingness to cut government spending by even one dollar, in spite of dire forewarnings about the impact that the federal debt will have on all Americans, is not only irresponsible, it is unforgivable. Yet, approximately 52% of Americans supported this man recently for reelection to a second term.

Obama has used the basest of all arguments to gain support, and that is to pit one American against another under the guise of fairness. And even his 2012 campaign slogan "Forward" has undeniable roots in socialist writings, as follows from the Washington Times, "*The slogan "Forward!" reflected the conviction of European Marxists and radicals that their movements reflected the march of history, which would move forward past capitalism and into socialism and communism. There have been at least two radical-left publications named "Vorwaerts" (the German word for "Forward"). One was the daily newspaper of the Social Democratic Party of Germany whose writers included Friedrich Engels and Leon Trotsky... Another was the 1844 biweekly reader of the Communist League. Karl Marx, Engels and Mikhail Bakunin are among the names associated with that publication. East Germany named its Army soccer club ASK Vorwaerts Berlin (later FC Vorwaerts Frankfort). Vladimir Lenin founded the publication "Vpered" (the Russian word for "forward") in 1905. Soviet propaganda film-maker Dziga Vertov made a documentary whose title is sometimes translated as "Forward, Soviet".*

In fact, Wikipedia has an entire section called "Forward" as the generic name for socialist publications. Yet the rabid Obama supporters, in spite of all of Obama's destructive policies and his communist leaning ideology, have ignored his associations and his radical past and have mindlessly defend him, no matter what the impact is to the country and to the world.

One of the stupidest lines of all time, and certainly one of the irresponsible lines ever uttered by an American president, is when Obama perhaps showed his socialist mindset the best by saying, "You didn't build that..." The entire quote is included below for accuracy:

> *There are a lot of wealthy, successful Americans who agree with me -- because they want to give something back. They know they didn't -- look, if you've been successful, you didn't get there on your own. You didn't get there on your own. I'm always struck by people who think, well, it must be because I was just so smart. There are a lot of smart people out there. It must be because I worked harder than everybody else. Let me tell you*

something -- there are a whole bunch of hardworking people out there. (Applause.)

If you were successful, somebody along the line gave you some help. There was a great teacher somewhere in your life. Somebody helped to create this unbelievable American system that we have that allowed you to thrive. Somebody invested in roads and bridges. If you've got a business -- you didn't build that. Somebody else made that happen. The Internet didn't get invented on its own. Government research created the Internet so that all the companies could make money off the Internet.

It would take too much space to detail how blind and stupid the above quoted statements are, because "yes, Mr. President" all businesses actually are built by individuals and in fact the government has not built one single thing during its plus 200 year history, including even the roads and bridges you refer to, because those were built for the government by private contractors. And, it is an urban myth that government invented the internet – it was invented at Xerox Corporation's PARC labs in Silicon Valley in the 1970's.

The "you didn't build that" quote in particular brings to light the socialist, collectivist, statist mentality of Obama and his thorough lack of understanding about what has made America great. America became the great country it is by the hard work of individuals, through their perseverance and dreams, and by their willingness to take risk, and it is the common people that made America great and they did so in spite of government, not because of it. This is something that Obama will never understand. And yes, Americans you did build that, and you should be supremely proud of yourself for having done so.

Obama is a sociopathic liar - even worse than Clinton, after whom the superlative for a liar was coined, a liar of Clintonian proportions or a Clintonian liar. For those of you Liberals who want to dispute the fact that Obama is a serial liar, just look up online the hundreds, if not thousands, of outright lies told by Obama to the American people. The only reason you want to dispute these facts is that you fell for these lies - lock, stock and barrel - and thus must defend Obama in spite of his constant lies to you. What a terrible position you have put yourself in.

The following are observations about Obama by Steve McCann of the American Thinker:

"Barack Obama is a product of 1960's radicalism. His parents, grandparents,

mentors, professors and, by his own admission, circle of friends were all disciples of Marxist thought and the tactics of societal revolution. Not only his formative years but virtually his entire life has been an immersion in this mindset -- a mindset which includes a deep seated animosity toward capitalism and individual freedom. Virtually all the despots of the twentieth century had the same philosophical convictions and intellectual backgrounds."

"What makes this belief system so popular among those who harbor megalomaniacal tendencies is the core tenet that the end justifies the means. With that simple phrase any tactic is permissible under the rubric that the true believers are pre-ordained to govern the people. Thus no lie is too egregious to tell, no strategy to destroy one's political enemies is out of bounds, and the creation of false crises and faux enemies is not only legitimate but essential. Any leader within government or the national community at large who is captive to this thinking, as Barack Obama has repeatedly revealed throughout his life and political career, must by necessity be devoid of ethics, integrity or morals."

"Nearly all the tyrants of the recent past had a unique capacity to mesmerize a large swath of the populace through ability to deliver a speech and create a cult of personality, aided and abetted by a media, if not state sponsored, then one willingly intimidated into doing the bidding of the exalted leader. This ability and extreme narcissism, which Barack Obama has in abundance, is another pre-requisite for despotism."

To us Conservatives, who use our minds to learn about problems and to investigate real solutions, the worst vision of America conceivable is the one we have had over the last five plus years, and that is of our fellow Americans, eyes glazed over and hands stretched out, walking aimlessly and chanting "Obama, Obama, change, change", like automatons or zombies beset upon and having become mindless by a great plague (e.g., "Imhotep, Imhotep, Imhotep"), or worse yet by someone like Obama who claims to be another American.

The road that Obama is bringing this country down is a dangerous one. After all, how do you think that dictators like Hitler came to power? Their ascents typically were started first by having the people buy into the rhetoric of class and racial warfare and religious hatred and bigotry. As an example of the danger Obama poses to America, in response to a 2013 New Year's Eve speech by Obama in which he was bragging about taxing the rich, Jeannie DeAngelis wrote, "*For four years, Barack Obama has worked diligently to disparage success. He has insidiously cultivated class envy and fueled it with ignorance using the false premise that the wealthy destroyed the nation and are deserving of monetary castigation.*

Clearly, Mr. Obama's persistence has worked, because the type of wicked satisfaction displayed in response to a sophomoric president boasting that the rich would be overtaxed reeked of a mob mentality reminiscent of a coliseum full of bloodthirsty spectators. Americans [Liberals] applauding the fact that other Americans [Conservatives] are to be punished by a leader for fabricated offenses helps one understand atrocities like the Romans cheering while their Christian neighbors were thrown to the lions merely for being Christian."

While Liberals scoff at the idea of Obama becoming a near dictator, people like Nancy Pelosi must give us all pause, because she and other Democrats want to give Obama the dictatorial power to raise the debt limit to infinity, as a start. Especially frightening is the empowerment given to Obama through Obamacare, as described below by Doug Book of the Western Center for Journalism:

> "*Though few Americans are aware of it, the unconscionable ObamaCare ruling of Chief Justice John Roberts stands to provide Barack Hussein Obama unlimited and fundamentally irrevocable power less than 2 years after the November election. … Obama will acquire the "legal" authority to select 15 individuals whose word will automatically become the law of the land. Within the 2500 pages of the comically-named Patient Protection and Affordable Care Act is cached the 2014 establishment of the Independent Payment Advisory Board. Nominated exclusively by the president, the 15 members of the Board will ostensibly be tasked with "…prevent[ing] per-enrollee Medicare spending from growing faster than a specified target rate." To accomplish this congressional mandate, ObamaCare has provided the Board with the authority to submit legislative "proposals" to Congress; proposals which will automatically become law unless both Houses AND the President agree upon and pass into law a substitute measure.*
>
> *In short, "the Board's edicts … become law without congressional action, congressional approval, meaningful congressional oversight, or being subject to a presidential veto." Moreover, citizens will have NO authority to challenge the Board's pronouncements in court, for ObamaCare "… specifically states that the Secretary [of Health and Human Service's] implementation of IPAB's proposals is not judicially reviewable." Therefore a group of presidential, POLITICAL appointees will have the practical power of shaping and imposing upon the American public, the laws of the land! For in addition to creating edicts loosely attached to Medicare and its myriad applications, in 2015 the IPAB will be permitted to impose price controls, taxes and "… ration care for all Americans whether the government pays their medical bills or not!" Thus even the Medicare stipulation will no longer be a practical deterrent to the Board's authority.*

Only "we the people" can stand against the tyrannical tendencies of government, and particularly those of Obama. And, all of us should indeed be mindful of Hitler's words, when he said, ""*The size of the lie is a definite factor in causing it to be believed, for the vast masses of a nation are in the depths of their hearts more easily deceived than they are consciously and intentionally bad. The primitive simplicity of their minds renders them a more easy prey to a big lie than a small one, for they themselves often tell little lies, but would be ashamed to tell big lies.*"

To put into perspective what has happened to the American economy under Obama, according to Patrick Burke of CNS News, "*Total federal spending on SNAP* [the federal food stamp program] *has increased each year during President Obama's first term in office. In FY 2009 -- when SNAP was still known as the "Food Stamp" program -- the government spent approximately $55.6 billion. By FY 2010, SNAP spending increased to nearly $70.5 billion. Between FY 2009 and FY 2012, SNAP's budget jumped by approximately $24.8 billion. According to an April 2012 report from the Congressional Budget Office, SNAP outlays increased by $42 billion between 2007 and 2011, and the number of SNAP participants increased by 70 percent.*

With regards to the number of federal employees under Obama, Representative Pete Sessions said on the House floor on July 30, 2012, "*The numbers are stunning, Over the time that President Obama has been in office, we have lost 2.5 million free enterprise system jobs, and, yet, 500,000 federal government jobs have been added in that period of time. The assault on the common man of this country is unrelenting by the Democrat majority.*"

Regarding federal employee pay relative to the private sector, according to the CBO, "*Overall, the federal government paid 16 percent more in total compensation than it would have if average compensation had been comparable with that in the private sector, after accounting for certain observable characteristics of workers*".

Already reported earlier was the significant increase in people receiving disability benefits under Obama. Also, according to The Foundry, "*The number of Americans dependent on the federal government has exploded over the past five years, reaching a record 67.3 million people, according to Heritage's annual Index of Dependence on Government. That means 1 in 5 Americans (21.8 percent) today receive some level of assistance from the federal government.*

Regarding total government dependency, according to Real Time Economics, "*49.1%: Percent of the population that lives in a household where at least one member received some type of government benefit in the first quarter of 2011.*" These numbers should give every American pause when it comes to government spending, the national debt and the relentless push towards socialism in America - a progression that has pushed the richest nation in the world towards becoming a destitute welfare state under the leadership of Obama and the Left.

Obama does not represent all Americans and he does not support the Constitution, in direct opposition to his sworn duty as President of the United States. Obama governs as if he is President of the ACLU and of every Liberal special interest group, and he does so in direct contradiction to the beliefs of at least half of the country's people. He does not understand, or he does not care to understand, that the federal government has certain responsibilities to all of its citizens. These responsibilities are those as summarized in the Preamble of the Constitution, as follows: "*We the People of the United States, in Order to form a more perfect Union, establish Justice, insure domestic Tranquility, provide for the common defence, promote the general Welfare, and secure the Blessings of Liberty to ourselves and our Posterity, do ordain and establish this Constitution for the United States of America*". And, as such, the federal government has only 17 enumerated powers – all others are reserved to the states.

Obama, as well as all others Liberals, incorrectly refers to the "General Welfare clause" of the Constitution as being the legal support for his radical agenda. However, there are only two places in the Constitution where the general welfare is mentioned. The first is in the Preamble, which legally is not part of the Constitution's laws, and the second is in Section 8, Powers of Congress which states, "*The Congress shall have Power To lay and collect Taxes, Duties, Imposts and Excises, to pay the Debts and provide for the common Defence and general Welfare of the United States*"; but these powers are subject to the 17 enumerated powers and as such no clause legally exists in the Constitution as an actual directive to do things for the "general welfare". Also, clearly the statement to "promote the general Welfare" means exactly what it says, and that is to *promote* the *general* welfare, which means at least to us Conservatives that government should promote the welfare of everyone – not just to provide for the affluence of certain groups at the expense of others, especially those groups that are chosen by Liberals in government on the basis of such twisted concepts as "fairness, equality and justice".

Under Obama and the Left, the warning written by James Madison may already be true if the Liberal interpretation of the general welfare "clause" is abused further; "*If Congress can employ money indefinitely to the general welfare, and are the sole and supreme judges of the general welfare, they may take the care of religion into their own hands; they may appoint teachers in every State, county and parish and pay them out of their public treasury; they may take into their own hands the education of children, establishing in like manner schools throughout the Union; they may assume the provision of the poor; they may undertake the regulation of all roads other than post-roads; in short, everything, from the highest object of state legislation down to the most minute object of police, would be thrown under the power of Congress... Were the power of Congress to be established in the latitude contended for, it would subvert the very foundations, and transmute the very nature of the limited Government established by the people of America."*

With regards to the recent scandals that the Obama administration is responsible for, including massive waste and fraud in the stimulus and "green" energy programs, Fast and Furious, Benghazi, the DOJ's investigations of AP and Fox News reporters, the EPA, IRS gate and the phone and internet tapping and spying on millions of Americans who have done nothing wrong, with more to come, all of this is evidence of what Conservatives have been warning about since Obama was first elected. All of this has happened because when you have a president who disdains the Constitution and American greatness he then may be prepared to do anything to promote his own power, no matter how lawless, like a common dictator, and worse yet then take no responsibility for the results of his actions and pass the problems off by always blaming others.

Mr. President, how could you allow Fast and Furious, with absolutely no way to track those guns, and then cover-up the details, very likely so that we would never find out that this program was intentionally orchestrated by you to put American-sourced guns in the hand of illegal Mexican cartels, just so you could justify additional anti-gun legislation? And with the resulting death of a US border agent from one of those guns, I would hope that you cannot sleep at night. But worse yet, to not send help to Americans under fire in Benghazi who were being brutally murdered while you slept, so you could cover-up your erroneous recent statements to the American people that Al Qaeda was destroyed, is a grievous dereliction not only of your sworn duty as Commander in Chief but of your responsibility to protect all Americans - especially those who work for you.

But the two most grievous examples of Obama's tyranny are the absolute attacks on our 1st Amendment rights as Americans, and that is the right of free speech, which includes political speech and freedom of the Press. While

Obama "joked" in a 2009 commencement speech at Arizona State University about using the IRS to target his enemies, the fact that this practice started in 2009 soon afterward, and is even continuing today, must be seen by any rational person as cause and effect, if not an outright smoking gun of Obama's duplicity (career government bureaucrats simply do not decide to do these things on their own and the scope of the interference is such that it had to come from the top). And let's be honest, the IRS targeting of Conservative groups is nothing short of illegal voter suppression, because it had the undeniable effect of keeping Tea Party Conservatives from organizing and raising money for the 2012 presidential election. As well, the domestic spying on millions of Americans through their phones and internet activities is absolutely comparable to Soviet/Nazi gulag tactics. The people responsible for all of these activities should go to jail, and for these atrocities Obama should be impeached. And with regards to the other atrocity of using the Department of "Justice" to investigate reporters, especially those who disagreed with Obama politically (i.e. they were Conservatives), there has never been an investigation of this type where reporters who are trying to find the truth are targeted for investigation– but rather historically leaks have been investigated for criminality by looking at the leakers, which in these cases are government employees under the Obama administration - the most leaked administration in history with many of the leaks coming straight from the top (aka, the Bin Laden raid, etc.).

Recently even the far, far left New York Times editorial board stated that Obama "*is proving the truism that the executive will use any power it is given and very likely abuse it.*" As well, they stated that the Obama administration "*has lost all credibility.*" This is a far cry from the adulation show towards Obama by the NYT in 2008 when the Times praised the candidate Obama's "*cool head and sound judgment*" and said he was "*putting real flesh on his early promises of hope and change*".

With regards to the recent Obama administration scandals, Liberals have been protecting Obama (no matter what) by saying, "He didn't know – you can't blame him." However, let's look at some interesting facts. The process set up in our government to provide a system of controls to investigate potential malfeasance and tyranny is the use of Inspectors General to ferret out government fraud, waste and mismanagement. These IG's are career government employees who are not politically appointed. Thus they have a reputation of being honest, unbiased and above political partisanship.

However, Obama has waged a until recently unreported war against the AG's, who are investigating the numerous reported and unreported scandals that his administration is involved with. This is yet another scandal that has not been reported by the mainstream press.

Obama's war against the Inspectors General has included not appointing people to vacant positions, or as highlighted by Congressman Darrel Issa, "*'This administration's failure to fill inspector-general vacancies has weakened the effectiveness of the inspector-general community, thus exposing American taxpayer dollars to waste, fraud and abuse.*" Also, Obama has dramatically cut funding for the Inspectors General, while increasing funding significantly for all other government functions, except Defense. But worse yet, the IG's who have been investigating Obama's fraud and abuse cases have been subjected to intimation and character assassination by his administration in thugary attempts to silence these people. As reported by Ed Lasky, a few examples of this behavior are as follows:

> *"Barack Obama's proxies have threatened Inspectors General on more than one occasion. Gerald Walpin ran afoul of the Obama team when he dared to report that a friend of Obama's was misusing government funds for personal expenses, meddled politically in a local election, and may have included hush money to women to keep them quiet about sexual harassment by him. What were Walpin's rewards for protecting taxpayers? His dismissal followed by heaps of personal abuse and accusations of mental illness*
>
> *He has company.*
>
> *The Inspector General at the OMB who reported on Obama's plans to slash his budget was told by officials there that they'd "make life miserable for him" if he complained about his budget being cut*
>
> *The Special Inspector General for Afghanistan Reconstruction reported that administration officials had pressured him to remain silent regarding the massive waste of funds and corruption associated with the program and that officials had tried to edit his report to remove anything that might embarrass the White House (presaging the Benghazi scandal). The abuse led to his resignation.*
>
> *The aforementioned Neil Barofsky was subject to scathing personal attack for exposing and disclosing massive waste and fraud in the Troubled Asset Relief Program. Jen Psaki, a spokeswoman for the 2008 campaign who had become the deputy*

communications director at the White House, engaged in such personal vituperation that it shocked old Washington hands. She accused Barofsky of trying to generate "false controversy" to "grab a few cheap headlines" and then continued with similar personal insults of Barofsky."

Recently, with regards to revelations that the government has been extensively spying on its own citizens via electronic means, Obama made the outrageous statement that Americans may need to give up some of their freedoms in exchange for security from terrorism. However, Conservatives believe that the president has no right whatsoever to decide what degree of freedom Americans can have, or should give up – those freedoms are defined not by Obama or the government but by the Constitution. The Fourth Amendment of the Constitution is very precise regarding unreasonable searches. The Fourth Amendment states: "*The right of the people to be secure in their persons, papers, and effects, against unreasonable searches and seizures, shall not be violated, and no Warrants shall issue, but upon probably cause, supported by Oath or affirmation, and particularly describing the places to be searched,, and the persons or things to be seized.*" Accordingly, because the NSA is conducting unrestricted and unwarranted searches of servers that belong to nine internet organizations, and more, their activities are a clear and undeniable violation of our Fourth Amendment law.

When the federal government engages in unconstitutional practices, wages warfare against some of its own citizens and even try's to silence its own internal watchdogs, these are not only clear abuses of power, they are unacceptable and dangerous practices that all American people should be outraged about and loudly be calling for Obama to be held accountable for. However, I have long said that Obama could sink to any level and do almost anything no matter how immoral or illegal and Liberals will just sink with him and defend him at any cost, like they did with Bill Clinton. This is one of the biggest differences between Liberals and Conservatives. Conservatives stand by their beliefs, while Liberals, in their own cognitive dissonance, blindly adhere to their religion and their idols.

While we Conservatives do not hate Obama, we do fear him and we hate what he is doing to this great nation. And, in particular we do not understand why any American who also believes in the greatness of this country and who wants a better life and future for himself or herself and for his or her children could ever defend and support Obama and his socialist and tyrannical ideologies. However, Obama is just a symptom of what Liberalism is doing to America, a consequence and not the creator, a result and not the initiator. With the rise of socialism in this country in the 1960's, someone like Obama was bound to come along sooner or later, so that the country could take a walk down the path towards collectivism, statism and personal greed, accompanied by the consequent corruption and government tyranny against the people that these archetypes foster. The only thing we as Americans can hope is, when we reach the bottom, and we will, at that point we will have learned our lesson and be amongst other nations in history that tried socialism, found that it did not work and returned, in our case to the teaching of our founding fathers and to the liberty and freedom loving people that we were so fortunately born to be.

37 THE RELIGION OF THE LEFT

Psychologists say that people need religion in one form or another and as such they will always invent a theology if they are not given one. So, while Liberals continue to secularize America by tearing down other religions, especially Christianity, they have in fact created their own religion, and that is the religion of Liberalism and of the Left. This religion tells Liberals how to think, how to act, what to say and what not to say, what to eat and what not to eat, who to like, who to hate and even what science to accept or not.

Robert Hall notes, *"I'm not the first to notice that the rise of thetic, unchurched, Godless Secular Humanists has resulted in liberals meeting this human need by converting Progressive Ideology into religious doctrine and admiration for Progressive leaders into unquestioning worship. Self-righteous calls for civility aside, this explains why they get so angry and vicious when you challenge any of their tenets. You are not disagreeing with them over policy. You are attacking the core of their religion, and their reaction is often the same as if you told a member of the Westboro Baptist Church that Jesus wasn't divine or a member of the Muslim Brotherhood that Mohammad was a fake. Blasphemy cannot be tolerated by fundamentalists of any stripe. To understand the Liberal religion, you must first understand that for them, intentions matter, not results for real people. If they can feel all warm and fuzzy about intentions, the actual outcomes are of no interest. Note that they find no cognitive dissonance when their principles collide with each other or with reality -- they just ignore it, in the grand tradition of many great religions."*

Examples of the dissonance between logic and reality in the Liberal religion include; you are a racist if you voted for Romney, but the 94% of Blacks that voted for Obama are not racists. The Christian religion is bad but Muslims are good, even though Muslims believe in no rights for women, a theocratic government and in killing homosexual people. Even though the government's own five year study published last month showed that the Head Start program has been completely ineffective, that does not matter and we should still fund that program because only the intention is important, not the result. Also, while George W. Bush was eviscerated by the Left for the Patriot Act, which was used sparingly for wireless searches, Obama gets a "attaboy" for not only not getting rid of the act but using it in much worse ways to warrantlessly spy on all Americans. Also, according to Hall, "*If Democrats and George Bush both looked at CIA intelligence and concluded there were WMDs in Iraq, the Democrats were using the best data they had, but Bush lied. When Obama and Susan Rice repeated CIA talking points about Benghazi (mysteriously changed by persons unknown) they weren't lying, they were repeating the intelligence they had. If Bush had said it was a spontaneous demonstration that would have been a lie, because Bush said it. If Obama said in 2008 that raising the debt ceiling was unpatriotic, and in 2011 that voting against raising the debt ceiling was wrong, both statements were true, because Obama said them*".

With regards to the debt ceiling, this is a quote from Obama in 2006, "*The fact that we are here today to debate raising America's debt limit is a sign of leadership failure. It is a sign that the US Government cannot pay its own bills. It is a sign that we now depend on ongoing financial assistance from foreign countries to finance our Government's reckless fiscal policies. Increasing America's debt weakens us domestically and internationally. Leadership means that, "the buck stops here.' Instead, Washington is shifting the burden of bad choices today onto the backs of our children and grandchildren. America has a debt problem and a failure of leadership. Americans deserve better.*" Today, however, Obama wants to increase spending and increase the debt ceiling ad infinitum, a true example of exact opposites, of cognitive dissonances, that are somehow allowable to the religion of the Left, as long as there are Liberal opposites.

The Liberal religion is also one of maximum bigotry and disdain, with outright hatred for, and disrespect of, Conservatives taught as being acceptable, no different in context than Muslims around the world being radicalized and taught to hate and persecute and even kill all non-believers. Jerry Shenk reminds us that, "*But the American left reserves its ugliest bigotry for Christians. When liberals speak or write about practicing Christians, especially evangelical Christians and, in this presidential election year, Mormons, no slander is unacceptable and no religious custom is off-limits. America's most prominent liberal has condescendingly denigrated Christians as "bitter clingers" to guns and religion. Liberals have (seriously) asked: "Do All Evangelical Leaders Believe Gays Should Be Put to Death?" They worry about reports that evangelicals are voting in record numbers. And they invent scenarios which question whether religious convictions resonate in the political arena. Every Christian, of any age or gender, is fair game for liberal animosity -- or left-wing redefini*tion."

Perhaps even more unconscionable, Bruce Walker writes, "*Because the sins of America are a religious article of faith to self-appointed black leaders and to self-appointed representatives of the female sex. And it is crucial that the sin is not racism or sexism, but specifically American (or, perhaps, Western) racism and sexism. There is a reason why black leaders long ignored the genocide in Sudan, in which whites were enslaving and murdering blacks: the whites in question were not American. There is a reason why feminist yawned when told about honor murders, female circumcision and the imprisonment of rape victims: the men in question were not American. The catechism of the Left is that America is evil. Hating America is a religion with radical feminists and militant blacks. It is a very bad religion. It is a religion immune to any cure. It is a religion founded upon lies. It is, in fact, more like a sick cult than any religion that normal Americans might follow. The greatness and goodness of America, as has so often been the case, is well defined by its mortal enemies."*

Jeffery T. Brown wrote the following regarding the religion of the Left:

> *Imagine a closed, regressive, sometimes violent culture. Freedom of thought brings punishment. One is not encouraged to consider alternative views. One's place in the culture is determined by circumstances of birth, and he can never be otherwise defined than by such things as race, gender, and social status. Strict adherence to the code is enforced at the risk of severe repercussions. Only carefully cultivated and proscribed beliefs are acceptable, and others are strongly, even violently discouraged. The beliefs are not grounded in truth, and often are the product of bigotry and overt prejudice. Intolerance and self-righteousness are hallmarks of the culture. Only dogmas approved by the hierarchy are permitted to be repeated. Those who chant and believe them, while punishing those who do not, are faithful. They are rewarded with acceptance, financial benefits, and even fame. They are held up as examples of virtue. They are deemed heroic.*
>
> *Opponents of the closed culture, however, are portrayed as dim-witted and slow-thinking, motivated by malice rather than wisdom or experience. Those who presume to profess a different faith have earned the privilege of being slandered and defamed by the culture. In this culture, religion and law are hopelessly blurred, so that the tenets of the culture's religion become policy. There are core beliefs which cannot be challenged or limited. Nonbelievers are infidels, and those who convert to conflicting beliefs are apostates... Those who do not adapt themselves to the closed culture are shunned, ostracized, publicly humiliated. They are treated as unworthy of existence alongside the virtuous practitioners of the closed culture. They are labeled the cult's "enemy".*
>
> *Perhaps, by now, you have concluded I was referring to an intolerant religious culture generating news by making its presence felt, and I was, but not the one you might have thought. I was speaking of the culture and religion of Liberalism, sometimes also called Progressivism. It has sacraments, such as abortion, socialized medicine, gay rights, green energy, wealth redistribution, gun prohibition, anti-Semitism and anti-Americanism, among others. Its high priests are treated as infallible. The religion actively seeks to reduce and replace all other religions with which it competes. It is enmeshed with the state, so that the religion and government have become virtually indistinguishable.*

The practitioners reveal themselves whenever they must defend the faith from any risk of exposure as a fraud. They wage their own form of jihad upon the nonbelievers and apostates.

We saw them advance the faith when they fabricated and then railed against an imaginary war on women, smearing and destroying as they crusaded. We watched them attempt and sometimes succeed in falsely criminalizing guns and gun ownership, at the expense of citizens who had done no wrongs. We have seen them willfully tell lies on the Senate floor, in White House press conferences, or on television news shows, regarding matters about which we already knew the truth. We saw them consciously conceal examples of their ideology fully realized, as with the Gosnell trial. We have seen them coldly attack and smear blacks and Hispanics who dared speak against their own repression and exploitation by the scions of the cult. We have seen them sprint from the muck whenever there is a tragedy they can falsely pin on their enemy and slither back when it is revealed that one of their own, or one they enabled, was the perpetrator.

However, we see them at their most dishonest, and their most vicious, when the high priests of their culture are in danger, as exemplified presently by the Benghazi hearings. Terms like "witch hunt" and "politicize" and "liars" are deployed to damage those who would expose cult leaders who have engaged in evil or criminal actions. Bomb-throwers limber up, eager to lob verbal incendiaries for the faith. Lies must be told loudly and in unison to drown out or erase the truth. The followers who accidentally learn about the proceedings must be reminded of their duty to the cult. To stray is to invite damnation. They must blind themselves to evidence and facts. Logic is an enemy. Believe only what the cult approves.

Those who saw the cult's malice practiced first-hand in Benghazi and at home, and who have the courage to risk their names and their life's work, are marked by a liberal fatwa. The integrity of truth-tellers must be publicly attacked. Their honor must be murdered. Defenders of the faith chant as one, and none can speak out against the lies and damage done to their own country unless they too wish to be afforded the 'apostate' treatment. Ideology trumps country. It trumps truth, integrity and honor. Ideology trumps God. The infidels must be destroyed. The cult comes first.

Many people that have become Liberals/Democrats in recent years, including some in my own family, have done so because of their bigotry against religion, and especially against the Christian religion, due to the fact that these same people were once religious but now are not, and like a reformed smoker are the first to viciously condemn what they once believed in and defended. But, interestingly, these people do not seem to realize that they have simply traded one religion for another – the religion of Christianity, which at least in the modern world teaches morality, virtue and goodness, for the religion of the Liberalism, which teaches hatred, bigotry and almost pagan-like adulation of Liberal dogmas and deities. This is because, as stated by Lloyd Marcus, "*Liberals always cater to man's lowest base instincts. They hate standards for behavior, labeling all rebuke of bad behavior as being intolerant and judgmental.*"

The illogic of the Liberal religion, where you will accept exact opposites without question and defend them endlessly, even those said by the same person, and where you will defend at any cost the immoral and the indefensible is an undeniable cognitive dissonance that is stunning in both its breadth and scope. The battle between Conservatism and the religion of the Left is really the difference between right and wrong, between good and evil and between light and love set against darkness and hate. For Liberals and their Leftist religion, the light of truth must be shunned and ignored so as to protect a political ideology that arose from the dark recesses of their own biased prejudices.

38 THE LIBERAL WAR ON WOMEN AND ON CHILDREN

While Liberals propagandize constantly that they alone are the real supporters of women and children in America and that Conservatives and Republicans "*Want women only for childbearing*" and "*Want to starve and kill your babies*", the real truth is the exact opposite. With regards to women, Liberals care nothing about women "rights" unless they are Liberal women. And, their litmus test of what constitutes support for female rights is whether or not a person or group is for abortion, or not. Said differently, the Left believes first and foremost that taking a stand *for* life instantly translates into opposition towards the female gender and thus anyone who is pro-life is by extension anti-women. As written by Jeannie DeAngelis, "*The right to abort the unborn is so precious to left-leaning women that they are even willing to overlook the fact that 50% of the fetuses losing their lives in abortion clinics are of the gender they believe Republicans are currently waging war against. The truth is that it's pro-choice women who discriminate; they're fine with liberal men being womanizers, perverts, and adulterers, and if women like Juanita Broderick consider what Bill Clinton did to her a "legitimate rape," then the men they admire can even be alleged rapists.*"

Similarly, if a man or a woman believes in the concepts of traditional marriage and family, they are to be considered anti-women and to be hated. And, of course all Christians are really anti-women in the minds of Liberals, even while those same Liberals strongly support Islamists, who are virulently anti-women. As such, Liberals are actually waging a war against women in America on a constant basis, or at least they are against women who have Conservative values. But, their war is really a war on all women, not just Conservative women, because every woman should have the same rights and receive the same respect whether they are Liberal or Conservative. If you think that this dichotomy does not exist, just look at the vile things said about Conservative women in politics over the last few years by Liberals, both male and female. And their war against women has real consequences, especially if you look at the many cases in the legal system where women were killed or raped but the perpetrators were let off or given lenient sentences by Liberal judges who believe that the "rights" of the criminals were more important than the rights of the female victims.

As has been discussed in many of the previous sections, Liberal policies are decidedly anti children. First and foremost is their support of abortion – the outright killing of children – which has actually been championed by some Liberals as "being good for the children" due to the fact that every child will then be a "wanted child". This of course is absolute nonsensical insanity, but notable also is Obama's restoration of American taxpayer funding for abortion groups in the third world. If Liberals truly loved children, they wouldn't be paying for the genocide of "brown babies" in the third world, and as well would more vociferously stand against China's forced abortion policies. Perhaps worse yet are the racial implications of abortion here in America, where Black women are nearly five times more likely to have an abortion than white women and where 79% of abortion clinics are located in minority neighborhoods.

The Liberal war on children includes championing single motherhood, with the previously mentioned societal problems for the children involved, letting criminals out of prison because of "poor" living conditions, some of whom will kill more children on the streets and championing policies that result in poor education and thus disadvantaged opportunities for children and for young people. Liberals also support laws that make getting a divorce simple and easy, irrespective of the impacts on children. And, Liberals support welfare and social policies that are hugely detrimental to children, including the willingness to take children away from their family and then to put them into homes other than where they belong or will flourish.

Even worse, on April 9, 2013 Melissa Harris-Perry, a Black professor at Tulane, and a host on MSNBC, shocked millions of Conservatives with her brazen TV promo spot that made even more crystal clear the statist belief that your children are not really yours at all – that they really belong to a "collective" or to the government – by saying, "*We have to break through our kind of private idea that kids belong to their parents or kids belong to their families and recognize that kids belong to whole communities.*" She also stated, "*We have never invested as much in public education as we should have because we've always had a private notion of children; your kid is yours and totally your responsibility. We haven't had a very collective notion of these are our children.*"

The radical Leftist viewpoint, that the state is really the owner of your children, is not new; it was perhaps most famously expressed in recent years by Hillary Clinton in her 1990s best-seller, "It Takes A Village." As well, statists/collectivists throughout history have said that not only should children belong to the state but that if you control them you control the future. As famously stated by the penultimate statist Adolf Hitler, who founded state-run youth camps that bore his name, "*He alone, who owns the youth, gains the future*". Chillingly, with the passage of H.R. 1388 in 2009, the Obama youth corps was created, with a stated purpose to "*combine the best practices of civilian service with the best aspects of military service.*" To this I say, huh???

So, if you are a Liberal because you believe in championing the "rights" of women and children, you might want to rethink your position. That is because it is us Conservatives who best understand these issues and afford women and children, not only true equal rights and protection, but more importantly true love and respect. And we Conservatives actually do believe that our children are ours; that they are both our responsibilities and as well they are our blessings.

39 WHY DO LIBERALS "THINK" THE WAY THEY DO?

So, why do Liberals in this country believe the exact opposite of our founding principles and of the Judeo Christian foundations to our national ethics and laws? And, why don't they seem to either understand or care about the reality of economics, about the importance of retaining liberty, or about self-determination and freedom? The phenomenon of the Liberal collective may have been explained best in 1936 by Walter Lippmann, who wrote in The Good Society:

"*... the people have had it fixed in their minds that the state possesses a magical power to provide an abundant life. They have come gradually to think that their expectations may be as great as their government is powerful; that the stronger the government, the more certainly it can satisfy their heart's desires. After a while, when the doctrine is completely dominant in the popular mind, a point is reached where men cease to feel that there is any vital connection between production and consumption, between work and wealth.*

It is no longer labor, but the law, the force of the state, the might of the government that is looked upon as the source of material well-being.

The belief in this miracle is due to an optical illusion. The power of the state, as such, produces nothing: it can only redistribute that which has been produced.

The optical illusion arises because men mistake for the production of wealth the enrichment of those who take the tolls".

Also, in Erich Fromm's 1963 piece "Disobedience as a Psychological and Moral Problem, he wonders, "*Why is man so prone to obey and why is it so difficult for him to disobey?*" He concludes: "*As long as I am obedient to the power of the State, the Church, or public opinion, I feel safe and protected. In fact, it makes little difference what power it is that I am obedient to. It is always an institution, or men, who use force in one form or another and who fraudulently claim omniscience and omnipotence. My obedience makes me part of the power I worship, and hence I feel strong. I can make no error, since it decides for me; I cannot be alone, because it watches over me; I cannot commit a sin, because it does not let me do so, and even if I do sin, the punishment is only the way of returning to the almighty power.*"

Similarly, as stated by Lyn Nofziger, "*The reason this country continues its drift toward socialism and big nanny government is because too many people vote in the expectation of getting something for nothing, not because they have a concern for what is good for the country. A better educated electorate might change the reason many persons vote. If children were forced to learn about the Constitution, about how government works, about how this nation came into being, about taxes and about how government forever threatens the cause of liberty perhaps we wouldn't see so many foolish ideas coming out of the mouths of silly men*".

Many of us have wondered about the "disease of the cities" in which, while 98% of the land mass in the United States is solidly Conservative and Republican, the people who live in our largest cities vote mostly liberally and support Democrats, even to their own ruin. This must be because there is something that is inherently different about large groups of people who live that close to one another – perhaps it is a fertile ground to breed the insanity and religion of the Left. Or, could this be because these people are part of a large collective? That collective thinking is a natural evolutionary result of their crowded condition? That, when they move from a farm or a rural setting where they have to be self-sufficient to survive, into a large city, they somehow lose a sense of self sufficiency and self-determination and begin to think collectively? Or is it more about demographics, where more people who are inherently of the type to think collectively somehow naturally gravitate towards the larger cities? The answers to these questions are not clear, but suffice it to say there are enormous differences between the large city dwellers and the rest of America in their political views.

40 WHAT YOU MUST HATE TO BE A LIBERAL

Liberals in America have a very long list indeed of what they are supposed to not only be against but to outright hate, as follows:

1. The United States Constitution
2. America
3. Conservatives
4. Free Market Capitalism, including:
    a. Any Large Corporation
    b. Small Businesses
    c. Pharmaceutical Companies
    d. Oil, Coal & Natural Gas Companies
    e. Tobacco Companies
    f. Wal-Mart
    g. McDonalds
    h. Microsoft
    i. Gun Manufacturers
    j. All Non-Union Businesses
    k. Corporate Profits
5. The Military & The Police
6. The Tea Party
7. The Internet
8. Guns & The NRA
9. Talk Radio
10. SUV's
11. Pledge of Allegiance
12. Right to Life Supporters
13. Traditional Marriage
14. Christianity
15. Christmas & the 4th of July
16. Capital Punishment
17. The Bible
18. Traditional Families
19. Doctors & Patients
20. Fox News
21. Home Schooling
22. Energy Independence
23. The Electoral College
24. American Exceptionalism

25. Boy Scouts and Girl Scouts (although maybe not the Boy Scouts now that they accept homosexuals).
26. The Second Amendment
27. The 10 Commandments
28. Israel
29. Football
30. Success
31. The Rich
32. Ethnic Humor
33. Churches
34. Family Values
35. Fiscal and Personal Responsibility
36. Tax Cuts
37. Global Warming Deniers
38. White Men & Conservative Black Men & Women, including:
    a. Anyone Named Bush (or Associated With Them)
    b. Ronald Reagan
    c. Sarah Palin
    d. Rush Limbaugh
    e. Mitt Romney (and Ann)
    f. Karl Rove
    g. Shawn Hannity
    h. Bill O'Reilly
    i. Richard Steele
    j. Michelle Bachmann
    k. Ron Paul
    l. Newt Gingrich
    m. Alan Keyes
    n. Glen Beck
    o. Margret Thatcher
    p. John Wayne
    q. Laura Ingram
    r. Ann Coulter

In short, Liberals are supposed to hate just about everything that is good and great about America.

41 EPILOGUE – A NATURAL PROGRESSION, THE STATE OF OUR REPUBLIC & MY RECOMMENDATIONS

From my start as a Liberal through my evolution to becoming a staunch patriotic Conservative American, I have indeed walked the path of both political extremes – a progression that I believe is due to being a mindless follower at the beginning to one where rational thought finally won out over selfishness and emotion. Perhaps that is a natural progression in life, from the heart to the mind, but for me it was inescapable, as I studied and traveled around the world and learned more, all the while realizing more and more every day that America is without a doubt the greatest country on Earth and how truly lucky we Americans are who live here. But I began to understand even further, that we all have a responsibility to protect the freedoms and liberty that we have, and that only government can take our freedom and liberty away, as is happening today.

And, I have come to appreciate more and more, and take the words of Thomas Jefferson to heart, who said, "*All tyranny needs to gain a foothold is for people of good conscience to remain silent*". I for one will remain silent no longer, because tyranny has already gained a strong foothold in this country, and all of our futures depend on us educating ourselves, asking questions, listening to other points of view and standing up for what we believe in. And most importantly, we should never accept what we are told by any politician, no matter the party affiliation, without first using our minds and examining what was said factually and intellectually. And in particular, we should never give freely of the freedom and liberty we have been so fortunately granted in this country, because as stated by Woodrow Wilson, "*Liberty has never come from the government. Liberty has always come from the subjects of government. The history of liberty is the history of resistance. The history of liberty is a history of the limitation of governmental power, not the increase of it*".

Also, while recent political discourse has conditioned us to believe and support one side versus another, Left vs. Right, Liberal vs. Conservative, or Democrat vs. Republican, the choice is actually a much simpler one to make, because as written by Ronald Reagan, "*You and I are told we must choose between a left or right, but I suggest there is no such thing as a left or right. There is only an up or down. Up to man's age-old dream -- the maximum of individual freedom consistent with order -- or down to the ant heap of totalitarianism. Regardless of their sincerity, their humanitarian motives, those who would sacrifice freedom for security have embarked on this downward path. Plutarch warned, 'The real destroyer of the liberties of the people is he who spreads among them bounties, donations and benefits".*

And, when it comes to government and ceding power to government for whatever reason, we should all heed the warning of Albert Jay Nock, "*Here is the Golden Rule of sound citizenship, the first and greatest lesson in the study of politics: You get the same order of criminality from any State to which you give power to exercise it; and whatever power you give the State to do things FOR you carries with it the equivalent power to do things TO you".*

For those of you who are Liberals, and who are Obama worshippers, just think about the platform you are supporting in the context of the following quote from William Boetcker, who timelessly said, "*You cannot bring about prosperity by discouraging thrift. You cannot help small men by tearing down big men. You cannot strengthen the weak by weakening the strong. You cannot lift the wage-earner by pulling down the wage-payer. You cannot help the poor man by destroying the rich. You cannot keep out of trouble by spending more than your income. You cannot further the brotherhood of man by inciting class hatred. You cannot establish security on borrowed money. You cannot build character and courage by taking away men's initiative and independence. You cannot help men permanently by doing for them what they could and should do for themselves".*

With regards to the state of our republic, it is the worst it has ever been and it is in undeniable crisis. The US federal government debt alone is now at $16.4 T and is rising by ~$4 B per day, with the government as recently as late 2012 borrowing 56 cents for every dollar it spent. It is impossible to see how the US can survive this increasing debt crisis, yet the government keeps on spending recklessly with no end in sight, especially in the latest fiscal cliff deal in which taxes for 80% of Americans were raised; but, incredibly, where spending was not cut by one penny but rather was increased by $ 4 T over 10 years. To put the federal debt in perspective, if we pay off the debt at a rate of one dollar per second it would take 541,200 years to zero the account. Our survival is further challenged by logarithmically increasing government regulations, all of which stymy the potential for taxable growth. With the reelection of Obama, the takers now outnumber the makers, the recipients now outnumber the producers and the low information voters now outnumber those who are informed. And, the words of Benjamin Franklin may have already come true, "*When the people find they can vote themselves money [from the treasury], that will herald the end of the republic*".

With the Democrat message of, "*we will take from the greedy rich and give to you the 'exploited poor*", it has become nearly impossible for Conservative Republicans to win any election, especially when the message they are trying to argue is the concept of personal responsibility versus the personal greed fostered by the Left. So, where does that leave America? I am afraid that it is already lost. And to you Liberals, there is a possibility that you may have already won. But if so, what you have "won" is the economic ruin of what was the greatest country in all of human history. The current national debt means that all of America will have a lower standard of living in the very near future. Triggers to economic demise include a falling US dollar, where foreign investors in our debt start to lose money due to currency imbalances, and as well the economic threat posed by any significant increases in real interest rates, whereby even the interest on the current debt becomes unaffordable. With the loose monetary policy of Obama, the US also faces the potential of very significant inflation in the near future. When this occurs, it will quickly erode household incomes and everyone's standard of living.

The impact of a US debt payment default has been predicted by many to be a catastrophic worldwide mega depression. In this scenario, all people will suffer, but those who will suffer most are those with low incomes and those who are already dependent on the government for their lives. This dependency is what has been fostered and fought for by the Left and the result of this enslavement truly will be appalling, both in this country and in others, because not even governments can escape the laws of economics for long, no matter that millions of greedy simpletons believe that all we have to do is to "tax the rich" to somehow continue with the current or higher levels of government spending. The greatest impact will also be on our children and our grandchildren and this is truly the very epitome of greed, where you are willing to take from your own children's futures to improve your own. But worse yet, these policies may be putting many of the world's children and poor into a situation where their very survival may be in question – and that is truly unconscionable.

Based on 2010 IRS data, the last year for which such data are available, the entire amount of taxes paid in 2010 by all individual filers was only $951.7 B, or about 42% of the total federal revenue (40% of the revenue is from payroll taxes and 9% is from corporate income taxes). To make up a $1.3 T annual deficit spending shortfall, every year the federal government would have to confiscate 100% of the annual income of all individuals with taxable earnings in the country over approximately $200,000 per year. Taking 100% of the taxable income from "millionaires", after taking into consideration the taxes they already pay, would only raise ~$580 B. And, when Obama talks about millionaires and billionaires, how many billionaires actually exist in the US? Remember that this question must be answered in terms of taxable annual income, because that is the basis upon which the federal government calculates taxes. The answer is that no one in the country makes a billion dollars a year - there are no billionaires in the US in terms of annual earnings - in spite of Obamas continuing reference to and denigration of this income "class".

The true cognitive dissonance of the Left is that, without extreme levels of confiscation, there simply is not enough money in the US to pay for the current tax and spend insanity of the Democrats, no matter what Obama and the Left try to tell you. And, with only 9% of the federal revenue from corporate income taxes, it is clear that we ought to decrease that tax from the current rate, which is the highest in the world at 34%, to a more competitive lower level, to say 20%, so as to promote the return of business to this country, with the consequential benefits of increased jobs and greater federal income from payroll taxes. But Liberals reject this proposal out of hand, because they refuse to decrease taxes by one penny, irrespective of real economic and social impacts and outcomes.

With regards to the health and wellbeing of our society, if we are to have any chance whatsoever of returning our country and our way of life back to Ronald Reagan's vision that, "*America is a shining city upon a hill whose beacon light guides freedom-loving people everywhere.*", my message to all Americans is to use your mind first and not just your heart, that elections and politics truly matter, and they matter greatly, and that there are tremendous differences between Conservatives and Liberals in this country. I have tried to highlight these differences herein, even though some will tell you that there are no differences between the political parties, in their attempt to act wiser and above the political process.

"Progressive" policies that I personally would support, but that would never be supported by Liberals are:

1. The federal government should get out of the race business. It should be considered morally wrong, if not illegal, to collect and use

government data on the basis of race, because that divisive data is not needed if we truly consider ourselves all to be Americans.

2. All environmental and other laws and taxes should be subjected to their own EIS, not an Environmental Impact Statement, but an Economic Impact Statement; such that the true economic impacts of those regulations can be understood before the passage of any new laws and taxes.
3. No law, regulation, tax or penalty can come out of any federal government agency, such as the EPA or others, without the approval of Congress.
4. The federal Department of Education should be abolished and education should be returned to the state/community level.
5. The use of czars by the executive branch and the abuse thereof should be reviewed and be strictly limited, because these positions are not voted on by the American people, nor are they subject to congressional review. The increasing use of czars, especially by Obama, to adjudicate power immediately below the presidential level substantially abuses the concept of the separation of powers, as outlined in the Constitution.
6. The abuse of Executive Orders by presidents, in particular Obama, should be reviewed, because the mistreatment of these powers goes beyond the concept of the Constitution, and is allowing what is comparable to executive branch dictatorship rule.
7. A balanced budget amendment should be adopted, except in times of war.

In summary, what are the consequential differences between modern-day Conservatives and Liberals? Simply put they are the diametrically opposed differences, respectively, between liberty and liberation, between individual freedom and servitude, between responsibility and greed, between respect and disdain, between rational thought and illogic, between individualism and collectivism, between respectful commonality and elitism, between honesty and deceit and between compassion and hatred. Conservatives believe that individualism and free will lead to self-determination, to productivity and to better opportunity for all mankind, whereas Liberals believe that individuals exist only as part of a collective, or as terrifyingly stated by Hillary Clinton, "*We must stop thinking of the individual and start thinking about what is best for society.*"

Keep in mind that the concepts codified in the Constitution are based on the best results of human history and that these concepts are timeless and enduring, no matter what Liberal's want as their "flavor of the moment" in terms of social experimentation. As stated by Abraham Lincoln, "*Don't interfere with anything in the Constitution. That must be maintained, for it is the only safeguard of our liberties.*" Also, as warned by Samuel Adams, "*The liberties of our country, the freedoms of our civil Constitution are worth defending at all hazards; it is our duty to defend them against all attacks. We have received them as a fair inheritance from our worthy ancestors. They purchased them for us with toil and danger and expense of treasure and blood. It will bring a mark of everlasting infamy on the present generation – enlightened as it is – if we should suffer them to be wrested from us by violence without a struggle, or to be cheated out of them by the artifices of designing men.*"

Also, be aware that it is easy to acquiesce to the popular views of others, but that it is much more difficult, and it takes effort and tremendous personal courage, to first really learn about the issues and then to stand up for your own personal convictions, particularly if they are not the same as the prevailing herd mentality. Remember that it is not only tolerable to be a Conservative, but it is admirable, and most importantly that the Conservative family is open to all members, no matter your race, "class" or creed. According to a recent Gallup poll, "*40% of Americans interviewed in national Gallup Poll surveys describe their political views as Conservative, 35% as moderate, and 21% as liberal.*" Again, remember what Lord Hailsham said, that "*Conservatism is not so much a philosophy as an attitude, a constant force, performing a timeless function in the development of a free society, and corresponding to a deep and permanent requirement of human nature itself.*"

However, if you call yourself a "moderate", I and others will have to ask, "Do you really believe in anything?" Because, to be a moderate one has to first find out where everyone else stands before deciding what position they support (i.e., the "moderate" position) and then by extension finally determine what you actually believe in. With regards to moderation, Thomas Paine famously said, "*A thing moderately good is not so good as it ought to be. Moderation in temper is always a virtue, but moderation in principle is always a vice.*"

Importantly, at times it is prudent for everyone to sit back and think about the different issues our country and our society face, even asking yourself, "Is that truly what I believe?", because we all change and change is good and the older we get hopefully the wiser we become, as I believe I have. It is especially important for you to think anew if you have been part of the state-sponsored public school system during the last 30 years or so, because you were subjected to a constant onslaught of Liberal enculturation, wherein you really never had a chance to think for yourself or were discouraged from doing so.

When you hear political rhetoric, particularly of the Left, use your mind and think about what is being said and then challenge it intellectually and vociferously. For example, when you hear a Liberal Democrat talk about government "investment", that actually means government spending with no plan or end in sight. When you hear the word "extreme" or "extremists", especially when applied to your fellow Americans, this means people who believe in the greatness of this nation, who believe in love and fairness and decency and who believe in fiscal responsibility and in the Constitution– in other words Conservatives who are really anything but extreme. And, when you hear Liberal's speak about "caring", think not about "compassion" but about "control". Liberals want you to believe that they "care", but as pointed out herein their economic and social policies are destroying this nation, they are structured toward mindless support and it is Conservatives who really care about people and about the country. This is because if you really care for someone there are times when the most responsible action is to help guide that person along a better path for themselves, as compared to destroying their free will and future through the imposition of destructive redistributive social policies.

Remember that morality still matters and never be afraid to admit that you love your country, no matter what others may say or the personal risk involved, because it should be your natural inclination, as well as your responsibility and your duty to do so as an American. In particular, research and understand that true freedom comes from hard work, education and productivity, and that those principles are not only your path to a better life and personal happiness for you and for all Americans, but they are your true responsibility to your children and to the rest of society.

And in particular, learn from the teachings of the great men and women quoted herein and elsewhere, and in doing so protect the freedoms we have left with all your strength, not only because those exceptional people founded and built this great country, but the only way to keep this country and by extension we the people who live in it truly free is to understand their wisdoms and to heed their warnings. As John Adams said, "*But a Constitution of Government once changed from Freedom, can never be restored. Liberty, once lost, is lost forever.*"

And lastly, but most importantly, please do not let it be the case, where we willingly lose the freedoms that our nation has fought so hard to preserve. Not only because it is in our self-interest and it is our duty to do so, as others have done for us, but it is our solemn obligation as Americans to safeguard those freedoms for our children, for our grandchildren and for all of those who are yet to be….

Not the end, but rather hopefully a new beginning…

Please note that copies of the Declaration of Independence and the Constitution of the United States are included in the flowing for reference by all.

42 THE DECLARATION OF INDEPENDENCE

(Adopted by Congress on July 4, 1776)

The Unanimous Declaration of the Thirteen United States of America

When, in the course of human events, it becomes necessary for one people to dissolve the political bands which have connected them with another, and to assume among the powers of the earth, the separate and equal station to which the laws of nature and of nature's God entitle them, a decent respect to the opinions of mankind requires that they should declare the causes which impel them to the separation.

We hold these truths to be self-evident, that all men are created equal, that they are endowed by their Creator with certain unalienable rights, that among these are life, liberty and the pursuit of happiness. That to secure these rights, governments are instituted among men, deriving their just powers from the consent of the governed. That whenever any form of government becomes destructive to these ends, it is the right of the people to alter or to abolish it, and to institute new government, laying its foundation on such principles and organizing its powers in such form, as to them shall seem most likely to effect their safety and happiness. Prudence, indeed, will dictate that governments long established should not be changed for light and transient causes; and accordingly all experience hath shown that mankind are more disposed to suffer, while evils are sufferable, than to right themselves by abolishing the forms to which they are accustomed. But when a long train of abuses and usurpations, pursuing invariably the same object evinces a design to reduce them under absolute despotism, it is their right, it is their duty, to throw off such government, and to provide new guards for their future security. --Such has been the patient sufferance of these colonies; and such is now the necessity which constrains them to alter their former systems of government. The history of the present King of Great Britain is a history of repeated injuries and usurpations, all having in direct object the establishment of an absolute tyranny over these states. To prove this, let facts be submitted to a candid world.

He has refused his assent to laws, the most wholesome and necessary for the public good.

He has forbidden his governors to pass laws of immediate and pressing importance, unless suspended in their operation till his assent should be obtained; and when so suspended, he has utterly neglected to attend to them.

He has refused to pass other laws for the accommodation of large districts of people, unless those people would relinquish the right of representation in the legislature, a right inestimable to them and formidable to tyrants only.

He has called together legislative bodies at places unusual, uncomfortable, and distant from the depository of their public records, for the sole purpose of fatiguing them into compliance with his measures.

He has dissolved representative houses repeatedly, for opposing with manly firmness his invasions on the rights of the people.

He has refused for a long time, after such dissolutions, to cause others to be elected; whereby the legislative powers, incapable of annihilation, have returned to the people at large for their exercise; the state remaining in the meantime exposed to all the dangers of invasion from without, and convulsions within.

He has endeavored to prevent the population of these states; for that purpose obstructing the laws for naturalization of foreigners; refusing to pass others to encourage their migration hither, and raising the conditions of new appropriations of lands.

He has obstructed the administration of justice, by refusing his assent to laws for establishing judiciary powers.

He has made judges dependent on his will alone, for the tenure of their offices, and the amount and payment of their salaries.

He has erected a multitude of new offices, and sent hither swarms of officers to harass our people, and eat out their substance.

He has kept among us, in times of peace, standing armies without the consent of our legislature.

He has affected to render the military independent of and superior to civil power.

He has combined with others to subject us to a jurisdiction foreign to our constitution, and unacknowledged by our laws; giving his assent to their acts of pretended legislation:

For quartering large bodies of armed troops among us:

For protecting them, by mock trial, from punishment for any murders which they should commit on the inhabitants of these states:

For cutting off our trade with all parts of the world:

For imposing taxes on us without our consent:

For depriving us in many cases, of the benefits of trial by jury:

For transporting us beyond seas to be tried for pretended offenses:

For abolishing the free system of English laws in a neighboring province, establishing therein an arbitrary government, and enlarging its boundaries so as to render it at once an example and fit instrument for introducing the same absolute rule in these colonies:

For taking away our charters, abolishing our most valuable laws, and altering fundamentally the forms of our governments:

For suspending our own legislatures, and declaring themselves invested with power to legislate for us in all cases whatsoever.

He has abdicated government here, by declaring us out of his protection and waging war against us.

He has plundered our seas, ravaged our coasts, burned our towns, and destroyed the lives of our people.

He is at this time transporting large armies of foreign mercenaries to complete the works of death, desolation and tyranny, already begun with circumstances of cruelty and perfidy scarcely paralleled in the most barbarous ages, and totally unworthy the head of a civilized nation.

He has constrained our fellow citizens taken captive on the high seas to bear arms against their country, to become the executioners of their friends and brethren, or to fall themselves by their hands.

He has excited domestic insurrections amongst us, and has endeavored to bring on the inhabitants of our frontiers, the merciless Indian savages, whose known rule of warfare, is undistinguished destruction of all ages, sexes and conditions.

In every stage of these oppressions we have petitioned for redress in the most humble terms: our repeated petitions have been answered only by repeated injury. A prince, whose character is thus marked by every act which may define a tyrant, is unfit to be the ruler of a free people.

Nor have we been wanting in attention to our British brethren. We have warned them from time to time of attempts by their legislature to extend an unwarrantable jurisdiction over us. We have reminded them of the circumstances of our emigration and settlement here. We have appealed to their native justice and magnanimity, and we have conjured them by the ties of our common kindred to disavow these usurpations, which, would inevitably interrupt our connections and correspondence. They too have been deaf to the voice of justice and of consanguinity. We must, therefore, acquiesce in the necessity, which denounces our separation, and hold them, as we hold the rest of mankind, enemies in war, in peace friends.

We, therefore, the representatives of the United States of America, in General Congress, assembled, appealing to the Supreme Judge of the world for the rectitude of our intentions, do, in the name, and by the authority of the good people of these colonies, solemnly publish and declare, that these united colonies are, and of right ought to be free and independent states; that they are absolved from all allegiance to the British Crown, and that all political connection between them and the state of Great Britain, is and ought to be totally dissolved; and that as free and independent states, they have full power to levy war, conclude peace, contract alliances, establish commerce, and to do all other acts and things which independent states may of right do. And for the support of this declaration, with a firm reliance on the protection of Divine Providence, we mutually pledge to each other our lives, our fortunes and our sacred honor.

New Hampshire: Josiah Bartlett, William Whipple, Matthew Thornton

Massachusetts: John Hancock, Samual Adams, John Adams, Robert Treat Paine, Elbridge Gerry

Rhode Island: Stephen Hopkins, William Ellery

Connecticut: Roger Sherman, Samuel Huntington, William Williams, Oliver Wolcott

New York: William Floyd, Philip Livingston, Francis Lewis, Lewis Morris

New Jersey: Richard Stockton, John Witherspoon, Francis Hopkinson, John Hart, Abraham Clark

Pennsylvania: Robert Morris, Benjamin Rush, Benjamin Franklin, John Morton, George Clymer, James Smith, George Taylor, James Wilson, George Ross

Delaware: Caesar Rodney, George Read, Thomas McKean

Maryland: Samuel Chase, William Paca, Thomas Stone, Charles Carroll of Carrollton

Virginia: George Wythe, Richard Henry Lee, Thomas Jefferson, Benjamin Harrison, Thomas Nelson, Jr., Francis Lightfoot Lee, Carter Braxton

North Carolina: William Hooper, Joseph Hewes, John Penn

South Carolina: Edward Rutledge, Thomas Heyward, Jr., Thomas Lynch, Jr., Arthur Middleton

Georgia: Button Gwinnett, Lyman Hall, George Walton

Source: The Pennsylvania Packet, July 8, 1776

43 THE CONSTITUTION OF THE UNITED STATES

PREAMBLE

We the People of the United States, in Order to form a more perfect Union, establish Justice, insure domestic Tranquility, provide for the common defence, promote the general Welfare, and secure the Blessings of Liberty to ourselves and our Posterity, do ordain and establish this Constitution for the United States of America.

ARTICLE I - THE LEGISLATIVE BRANCH

Section 1 - The Legislature

All legislative Powers herein granted shall be vested in a Congress of the United States, which shall consist of a Senate and House of Representatives.

Section 2 - The House

The House of Representatives shall be composed of Members chosen every second Year by the People of the several States, and the Electors in each State shall have the Qualifications requisite for Electors of the most numerous Branch of the State Legislature.

No Person shall be a Representative who shall not have attained to the Age of twenty five Years, and been seven Years a Citizen of the United States, and who shall not, when elected, be an Inhabitant of that State in which he shall be chosen.

(Representatives and direct Taxes shall be apportioned among the several States which may be included within this Union, according to their respective Numbers, which shall be determined by adding to the whole Number of free Persons, including those bound to Service for a Term of Years, and excluding Indians not taxed, three fifths of all other Persons.) **(The previous sentence in parentheses was modified by the 14th Amendment, section 2.)** The actual Enumeration shall be made within three Years after the first Meeting of the Congress of the United States, and within every subsequent Term of ten Years, in such Manner as they shall by Law direct. The Number of Representatives shall not exceed one for every thirty Thousand, but each State shall have at Least one Representative; and until such enumeration shall be made, the State of New Hampshire shall be entitled to chuse three, Massachusetts eight, Rhode Island and Providence Plantations one, Connecticut five, New York six, New Jersey four,

Pennsylvania eight, Delaware one, Maryland six, Virginia ten, North Carolina five, South Carolina five and Georgia three.

When vacancies happen in the Representation from any State, the Executive Authority thereof shall issue Writs of Election to fill such Vacancies.

The House of Representatives shall chuse their Speaker and other Officers; and shall have the sole Power of Impeachment.

Section 3 - The Senate

The Senate of the United States shall be composed of two Senators from each State, *(chosen by the Legislature thereof,)* **(The preceding words in parentheses superseded by 17th Amendment, section 1.)** for six Years; and each Senator shall have one Vote.

Immediately after they shall be assembled in Consequence of the first Election, they shall be divided as equally as may be into three Classes. The Seats of the Senators of the first Class shall be vacated at the Expiration of the second Year, of the second Class at the Expiration of the fourth Year, and of the third Class at the Expiration of the sixth Year, so that one third may be chosen every second Year; *(and if Vacancies happen by Resignation, or otherwise, during the Recess of the Legislature of any State, the Executive thereof may make temporary Appointments until the next Meeting of the Legislature, which shall then fill such Vacancies.)* **(The preceding words in parentheses were superseded by the 17th Amendment, section 2.)**

No person shall be a Senator who shall not have attained to the Age of thirty Years, and been nine Years a Citizen of the United States, and who shall not, when elected, be an Inhabitant of that State for which he shall be chosen.

The Vice President of the United States shall be President of the Senate, but shall have no Vote, unless they be equally divided.

The Senate shall chuse their other Officers, and also a President pro tempore, in the absence of the Vice President, or when he shall exercise the Office of President of the United States.

The Senate shall have the sole Power to try all Impeachments. When sitting for that Purpose, they shall be on Oath or Affirmation. When the President of the United States is tried, the Chief Justice shall preside: And no Person shall be convicted without the Concurrence of two thirds of the Members present.

Judgment in Cases of Impeachment shall not extend further than to removal from Office, and disqualification to hold and enjoy any Office of honor, Trust or Profit under the United States: but the Party convicted shall nevertheless be liable and subject to Indictment, Trial, Judgment and Punishment, according to Law.

Section 4 - Elections, Meetings

The Times, Places and Manner of holding Elections for Senators and Representatives, shall be prescribed in each State by the Legislature thereof; but the Congress may at any time by Law make or alter such Regulations, except as to the Place of Chusing Senators.

The Congress shall assemble at least once in every Year, and such Meeting shall *(be on the first Monday in December,)* **(The preceding words in parentheses were superseded by the 20th Amendment, section 2.)** unless they shall by Law appoint a different Day.

Section 5 - Membership, Rules, Journals, Adjournment

Each House shall be the Judge of the Elections, Returns and Qualifications of its own Members, and a Majority of each shall constitute a Quorum to do Business; but a smaller number may adjourn from day to day, and may be authorized to compel the Attendance of absent Members, in such Manner, and under such Penalties as each House may provide.

Each House may determine the Rules of its Proceedings, punish its Members for disorderly Behavior, and, with the Concurrence of two-thirds, expel a Member.

Each House shall keep a Journal of its Proceedings, and from time to time publish the same, excepting such Parts as may in their Judgment require Secrecy; and the Yeas and Nays of the Members of either House on any question shall, at the Desire of one fifth of those Present, be entered on the Journal.

Neither House, during the Session of Congress, shall, without the Consent of the other, adjourn for more than three days, nor to any other Place than that in which the two Houses shall be sitting.

Section 6 - Compensation

(The Senators and Representatives shall receive a Compensation for their Services, to be ascertained by Law, and paid out of the Treasury of the United States.) **(The preceding words in parentheses were modified by the 27th Amendment.)** They shall in all Cases, except Treason, Felony and Breach of the Peace, be privileged from Arrest during their Attendance at the Session of their respective Houses, and in going to and returning from the same; and for any Speech or Debate in either House, they shall not be questioned in any other Place.

No Senator or Representative shall, during the Time for which he was elected, be appointed to any civil Office under the Authority of the United States which shall have been created, or the Emoluments whereof shall have been increased during such time; and no Person holding any Office under the United States, shall be a Member of either House during his Continuance in Office.

Section 7 - Revenue Bills, Legislative Process, Presidential Veto

All bills for raising Revenue shall originate in the House of Representatives; but the Senate may propose or concur with Amendments as on other Bills.

Every Bill which shall have passed the House of Representatives and the Senate, shall, before it become a Law, be presented to the President of the United States; If he approve he shall sign it, but if not he shall return it, with his Objections to that House in which it shall have originated, who shall enter the Objections at large on their Journal, and proceed to reconsider it. If after such Reconsideration two thirds of that House shall agree to pass the Bill, it shall be sent, together with the Objections, to the other House, by which it shall likewise be reconsidered, and if approved by two thirds of that House, it shall become a Law. But in all such Cases the Votes of both Houses shall be determined by Yeas and Nays, and the Names of the Persons voting for and against the Bill shall be entered on the Journal of each House respectively. If any Bill shall not be returned by the President within ten Days (Sundays excepted) after it shall have been presented to him, the Same shall be a Law, in like Manner as if he had signed it, unless the Congress by their Adjournment prevent its Return, in which Case it shall not be a Law.

Every Order, Resolution, or Vote to which the Concurrence of the Senate and House of Representatives may be necessary (except on a question of Adjournment) shall be presented to the President of the United States; and before the Same shall take Effect, shall be approved by him, or being disapproved by him, shall be repassed by two thirds of the Senate and House of Representatives, according to the Rules and Limitations prescribed in the Case of a Bill.

Section 8 - Powers of Congress

The Congress shall have Power To lay and collect Taxes, Duties, Imposts and Excises, to pay the Debts and provide for the common Defence and general Welfare of the United States; but all Duties, Imposts and Excises shall be uniform throughout the United States;

To borrow money on the credit of the United States;

To regulate Commerce with foreign Nations, and among the several States, and with the Indian Tribes;

To establish an uniform Rule of Naturalization, and uniform Laws on the subject of Bankruptcies throughout the United States;

To coin Money, regulate the Value thereof, and of foreign Coin, and fix the Standard of Weights and Measures;

To provide for the Punishment of counterfeiting the Securities and current Coin of the United States;

To establish Post Offices and Post Roads;

To promote the Progress of Science and useful Arts, by securing for limited Times to Authors and Inventors the exclusive Right to their respective Writings and Discoveries;

To constitute Tribunals inferior to the supreme Court;

To define and punish Piracies and Felonies committed on the high Seas, and Offenses against the Law of Nations;

To declare War, grant Letters of Marque and Reprisal, and make Rules concerning Captures on Land and Water;

To raise and support Armies, but no Appropriation of Money to that Use shall be for a longer Term than two Years;

To provide and maintain a Navy;

To make Rules for the Government and Regulation of the land and naval Forces;

To provide for calling forth the Militia to execute the Laws of the Union, suppress Insurrections and repel Invasions;

To provide for organizing, arming, and disciplining, the Militia, and for governing such Part of them as may be employed in the Service of the United States, reserving to the States respectively, the Appointment of the Officers, and the Authority of training the Militia according to the discipline prescribed by Congress;

To exercise exclusive Legislation in all Cases whatsoever, over such District (not exceeding ten Miles square) as may, by Cession of particular States, and the acceptance of Congress, become the Seat of the Government of the United States, and to exercise like Authority over all Places purchased by the Consent of the Legislature of the State in which the Same shall be, for the Erection of Forts, Magazines, Arsenals, dock-Yards, and other needful Buildings; And

To make all Laws which shall be necessary and proper for carrying into Execution the foregoing Powers, and all other Powers vested by this Constitution in the Government of the United States, or in any Department or Officer thereof.

Section 9 - Limits on Congress

The Migration or Importation of such Persons as any of the States now existing shall think proper to admit, shall not be prohibited by the Congress prior to the Year one thousand eight hundred and eight, but a tax or duty may be imposed on such Importation, not exceeding ten dollars for each Person.

The privilege of the Writ of Habeas Corpus shall not be suspended, unless when in Cases of Rebellion or Invasion the public Safety may require it.

No Bill of Attainder or ex post facto Law shall be passed.

(No capitation, or other direct, Tax shall be laid, unless in Proportion to the Census or Enumeration herein before directed to be taken.) **(Section in parentheses clarified by the 16th Amendment.)**

No Tax or Duty shall be laid on Articles exported from any State.

No Preference shall be given by any Regulation of Commerce or Revenue to the Ports of one State over those of another: nor shall Vessels bound to, or from, one State, be obliged to enter, clear, or pay Duties in another.

No Money shall be drawn from the Treasury, but in Consequence of Appropriations made by Law; and a regular Statement and Account of the Receipts and Expenditures of all public Money shall be published from time to time.

No Title of Nobility shall be granted by the United States: And no Person holding any Office of Profit or Trust under them, shall, without the Consent of the Congress, accept of any present, Emolument, Office, or Title, of any kind whatever, from any King, Prince or foreign State.

Section 10 - Powers prohibited of States

No State shall enter into any Treaty, Alliance, or Confederation; grant Letters of Marque and Reprisal; coin Money; emit Bills of Credit; make any Thing but gold and silver Coin a Tender in Payment of Debts; pass any Bill of Attainder, ex post facto Law, or Law impairing the Obligation of Contracts, or grant any Title of Nobility.

No State shall, without the Consent of the Congress, lay any Imposts or Duties on Imports or Exports, except what may be absolutely necessary for executing it's inspection Laws: and the net Produce of all Duties and Imposts, laid by any State on Imports or Exports, shall be for the Use of the Treasury of the United States; and all such Laws shall be subject to the Revision and Controul of the Congress.

No State shall, without the Consent of Congress, lay any duty of Tonnage, keep Troops, or Ships of War in time of Peace, enter into any Agreement or Compact with another State, or with a foreign Power, or engage in War, unless actually invaded, or in such imminent Danger as will not admit of delay.

ARTICLE II - THE EXECUTIVE BRANCH

Section 1 - The President

The executive Power shall be vested in a President of the United States of America. He shall hold his Office during the Term of four Years, and, together with the Vice-President chosen for the same Term, be elected, as follows:

Each State shall appoint, in such Manner as the Legislature thereof may direct, a Number of Electors, equal to the whole Number of Senators and Representatives to which the State may be entitled in the Congress: but no Senator or Representative, or Person holding an Office of Trust or Profit under the United States, shall be appointed an Elector.

(The Electors shall meet in their respective States, and vote by Ballot for two persons, of whom one at least shall not lie an Inhabitant of the same State with themselves. And they shall make a List of all the Persons voted for, and of the Number of Votes for each; which List they shall sign and certify, and transmit sealed to the Seat of the Government of the United States, directed to the President of the Senate. The President of the Senate shall, in the Presence of the Senate and House of Representatives, open all the Certificates, and the Votes shall then be counted. The Person having the greatest Number of Votes shall be the President, if such Number be a Majority of the whole Number of Electors appointed; and if there be more than one who have such Majority, and have an equal Number of Votes, then the House of Representatives shall immediately chuse by Ballot one of them for President; and if no Person have a Majority, then from the five highest on the List the said House shall in like Manner chuse the President. But in chusing the President, the Votes shall be taken by States, the Representation from each State having one Vote; a quorum for this Purpose shall consist of a Member or Members from two-thirds of the States, and a Majority of all the States shall be necessary to a Choice. In every Case, after the Choice of the President, the Person having the greatest Number of Votes of the Electors shall be the Vice President. But if there should remain two or more who have equal Votes, the Senate shall chuse from them by Ballot the Vice-President.) **(This clause in parentheses was superseded by the 12th Amendment.)**

The Congress may determine the Time of chusing the Electors, and the Day on which they shall give their Votes; which Day shall be the same throughout the United States.

No person except a natural born Citizen, or a Citizen of the United States, at the time of the Adoption of this Constitution, shall be eligible to the Office of President; neither shall any Person be eligible to that Office who shall not have attained to the Age of thirty-five Years, and been fourteen Years a Resident within the United States.

(In Case of the Removal of the President from Office, or of his Death, Resignation, or Inability to discharge the Powers and Duties of the said Office, the same shall devolve on the Vice President, and the Congress may by Law provide for the Case of Removal, Death, Resignation or Inability, both of the President and Vice President, declaring what Officer shall then act as President, and such Officer shall act accordingly, until the Disability be removed, or a President shall be elected.) **(This clause in parentheses has been modified by the 20th and 25th Amendments.)**

The President shall, at stated Times, receive for his Services, a Compensation, which shall neither be increased nor diminished during the Period for which he shall have been elected, and he shall not receive within that Period any other Emolument from the United States, or any of them.

Before he enter on the Execution of his Office, he shall take the following Oath or Affirmation:

"I do solemnly swear (or affirm) that I will faithfully execute the Office of President of the United States, and will to the best of my Ability, preserve, protect and defend the Constitution of the United States."

Section 2 - Civilian Power over Military, Cabinet, Pardon Power, Appointments

The President shall be Commander in Chief of the Army and Navy of the United States, and of the Militia of the several States, when called into the actual Service of the United States; he may require the Opinion, in writing, of the principal Officer in each of the executive Departments, upon any subject relating to the Duties of their respective Offices, and he shall have Power to Grant Reprieves and Pardons for Offenses against the United States, except in Cases of Impeachment.

He shall have Power, by and with the Advice and Consent of the Senate, to make Treaties, provided two thirds of the Senators present concur; and he shall nominate, and by and with the Advice and Consent of the Senate, shall appoint Ambassadors, other public Ministers and Consuls, Judges of the supreme Court, and all other Officers of the United States, whose Appointments are not herein otherwise provided for, and which shall be established by Law: but the Congress may by Law vest the Appointment of such inferior Officers, as they think proper, in the President alone, in the Courts of Law, or in the Heads of Departments.

The President shall have Power to fill up all Vacancies that may happen during the Recess of the Senate, by granting Commissions which shall expire at the End of their next Session.

Section 3 - State of the Union, Convening Congress

He shall from time to time give to the Congress Information of the State of the Union, and recommend to their Consideration such Measures as he shall judge necessary and expedient; he may, on extraordinary Occasions, convene both Houses, or either of them, and in Case of Disagreement between them, with Respect to the Time of Adjournment, he may adjourn them to such Time as he shall think proper; he shall receive Ambassadors and other public Ministers; he shall take Care that the Laws be faithfully executed, and shall Commission all the Officers of the United States.

Section 4 - Disqualification

The President, Vice President and all civil Officers of the United States, shall be removed from Office on Impeachment for, and Conviction of, Treason, Bribery, or other high Crimes and Misdemeanors.

ARTICLE III - THE JUDICIAL BRANCH

Section 1 - Judicial powers

The judicial Power of the United States, shall be vested in one supreme Court, and in such inferior Courts as the Congress may from time to time ordain and establish. The Judges, both of the supreme and inferior Courts, shall hold their Offices during good Behavior, and shall, at stated Times, receive for their Services a Compensation which shall not be diminished during their Continuance in Office.

Section 2 - Trial by Jury, Original Jurisdiction, Jury Trials

(The judicial Power shall extend to all Cases, in Law and Equity, arising under this Constitution, the Laws of the United States, and Treaties made, or which shall be made, under their Authority; to all Cases affecting Ambassadors, other public Ministers and Consuls; to all Cases of admiralty and maritime Jurisdiction; to Controversies to which the United States shall be a Party; to Controversies between two or more States; between a State and Citizens of another State; between Citizens of different States; between Citizens of the same State claiming Lands under Grants of different States, and between a State, or the Citizens thereof, and foreign States, Citizens or Subjects.) **(This section in parentheses is modified by the 11th Amendment.)**

In all Cases affecting Ambassadors, other public Ministers and Consuls, and those in which a State shall be Party, the supreme Court shall have original Jurisdiction. In all the other Cases before mentioned, the supreme Court shall have appellate Jurisdiction, both as to Law and Fact, with such Exceptions, and under such Regulations as the Congress shall make.

The Trial of all Crimes, except in Cases of Impeachment, shall be by Jury; and such Trial shall be held in the State where the said Crimes shall have been committed; but when not committed within any State, the Trial shall be at such Place or Places as the Congress may by Law have directed.

Section 3 - Treason

Treason against the United States, shall consist only in levying War against them, or in adhering to their Enemies, giving them Aid and Comfort. No Person shall be convicted of Treason unless on the Testimony of two Witnesses to the same overt Act, or on Confession in open Court.

The Congress shall have power to declare the Punishment of Treason, but no Attainder of Treason shall work Corruption of Blood, or Forfeiture except during the Life of the Person attainted.

ARTICLE IV - THE STATES

Section 1 - Each State to Honor all others

Full Faith and Credit shall be given in each State to the public Acts, Records, and judicial Proceedings of every other State. And the Congress may by general Laws prescribe the Manner in which such Acts, Records and Proceedings shall be proved, and the Effect thereof.

Section 2 - State citizens, Extradition

The Citizens of each State shall be entitled to all Privileges and Immunities of Citizens in the several States.

A Person charged in any State with Treason, Felony, or other Crime, who shall flee from Justice, and be found in another State, shall on demand of the executive Authority of the State from which he fled, be delivered up, to be removed to the State having Jurisdiction of the Crime.

(No Person held to Service or Labour in one State, under the Laws thereof, escaping into another, shall, in Consequence of any Law or Regulation therein, be discharged from such Service or Labour, But shall be delivered up on Claim of the Party to whom such Service or Labour may be due.) **(This clause in parentheses is superseded by the 13th Amendment.)**

Section 3 - New States

New States may be admitted by the Congress into this Union; but no new States shall be formed or erected within the Jurisdiction of any other State; nor any State be formed by the Junction of two or more States, or parts of States, without the Consent of the Legislatures of the States concerned as well as of the Congress.

The Congress shall have Power to dispose of and make all needful Rules and Regulations respecting the Territory or other Property belonging to the United States; and nothing in this Constitution shall be so construed as to Prejudice any Claims of the United States, or of any particular State.

Section 4 - Republican government

The United States shall guarantee to every State in this Union a Republican Form of Government, and shall protect each of them against Invasion; and on Application of the Legislature, or of the Executive (when the Legislature cannot be convened) against domestic Violence.

ARTICLE V - AMENDMENT

The Congress, whenever two thirds of both Houses shall deem it necessary, shall propose Amendments to this Constitution, or, on the Application of the Legislatures of two thirds of the several States, shall call a Convention for proposing Amendments, which, in either Case, shall be valid to all Intents and Purposes, as part of this Constitution, when ratified by the Legislatures of three fourths of the several States, or by Conventions in three fourths thereof, as the one or the other Mode of Ratification may be proposed by the Congress; Provided that no Amendment which may be made prior to the Year One thousand eight hundred and eight shall in any Manner

affect the first and fourth Clauses in the Ninth Section of the first Article; and that no State, without its Consent, shall be deprived of its equal Suffrage in the Senate.

ARTICLE VI - DEBTS, SUPREMACY, OATHS

All Debts contracted and Engagements entered into, before the Adoption of this Constitution, shall be as valid against the United States under this Constitution, as under the Confederation.

This Constitution, and the Laws of the United States which shall be made in Pursuance thereof; and all Treaties made, or which shall be made, under the Authority of the United States, shall be the supreme Law of the Land; and the Judges in every State shall be bound thereby, any Thing in the Constitution or Laws of any State to the Contrary notwithstanding.

The Senators and Representatives before mentioned, and the Members of the several State Legislatures, and all executive and judicial Officers, both of the United States and of the several States, shall be bound by Oath or Affirmation, to support this Constitution; but no religious Test shall ever be required as a Qualification to any Office or public Trust under the United States.

ARTICLE VII - RATIFICATION

The Ratification of the Conventions of nine States, shall be sufficient for the Establishment of this Constitution between the States so ratifying the Same.

Done in Convention by the Unanimous Consent of the States present the Seventeenth Day of September in the Year of our Lord one thousand seven hundred and Eighty seven and of the Independence of the United States of America the Twelfth. In Witness whereof We have hereunto subscribed our Names.

Go Washington - President and deputy from Virginia

New Hampshire - John Langdon, Nicholas Gilman

Massachusetts - Nathaniel Gorham, Rufus King

Connecticut - Wm Saml Johnson, Roger Sherman

New York - Alexander Hamilton

New Jersey - Wil Livingston, David Brearley, Wm Paterson, Jona. Dayton

Pensylvania - B Franklin, Thomas Mifflin, Robt Morris, Geo. Clymer, Thos FitzSimons, Jared Ingersoll, James Wilson, Gouv Morris

Delaware - Geo. Read, Gunning Bedford jun, John Dickinson, Richard Bassett, Jaco. Broom

Maryland - James McHenry, Dan of St Tho Jenifer, Danl Carroll

Virginia - John Blair, James Madison Jr.

North Carolina - Wm Blount, Richd Dobbs Spaight, Hu Williamson

South Carolina - J. Rutledge, Charles Cotesworth Pinckney, Charles Pinckney, Pierce Butler

Georgia - William Few, Abr Baldwin

Attest: William Jackson, Secretary

44 AMENDMENTS TO THE CONSTITUTION OF THE UNITED STATES

The following are the Amendments to the Constitution. The first ten Amendments collectively are commonly known as the Bill of Rights.

Amendment 1 - Freedom of Religion, Press, Expression. Ratified 12/15/1791.

Congress shall make no law respecting an establishment of religion, or prohibiting the free exercise thereof; or abridging the freedom of speech, or of the press; or the right of the people peaceably to assemble, and to petition the Government for a redress of grievances.

Amendment 2 - Right to Bear Arms. Ratified 12/15/1791.

A well regulated Militia, being necessary to the security of a free State, the right of the people to keep and bear Arms, shall not be infringed.

Amendment 3 - Quartering of Soldiers. Ratified 12/15/1791.

No Soldier shall, in time of peace be quartered in any house, without the consent of the Owner, nor in time of war, but in a manner to be prescribed by law.

Amendment 4 - Search and Seizure. Ratified 12/15/1791.

The right of the people to be secure in their persons, houses, papers, and effects, against unreasonable searches and seizures, shall not be violated, and no Warrants shall issue, but upon probable cause, supported by Oath or affirmation, and particularly describing the place to be searched, and the persons or things to be seized.

Amendment 5 - Trial and Punishment, Compensation for Takings. Ratified 12/15/1791.

No person shall be held to answer for a capital, or otherwise infamous crime, unless on a presentment or indictment of a Grand Jury, except in cases arising in the land or naval forces, or in the Militia, when in actual service in time of War or public danger; nor shall any person be subject for the same offense to be twice put in jeopardy of life or limb; nor shall be compelled in any criminal case to be a witness against himself, nor be deprived of life, liberty, or property, without due process of law; nor shall private property be taken for public use, without just compensation.

Amendment 6 - Right to Speedy Trial, Confrontation of Witnesses. Ratified 12/15/1791.

In all criminal prosecutions, the accused shall enjoy the right to a speedy and public trial, by an impartial jury of the State and district wherein the crime shall have been committed, which district shall have been previously ascertained by law, and to be informed of the nature and cause of the accusation; to be confronted with the witnesses against him; to have compulsory process for obtaining witnesses in his favor, and to have the Assistance of Counsel for his defence.

Amendment 7 - Trial by Jury in Civil Cases. Ratified 12/15/1791.

In Suits at common law, where the value in controversy shall exceed twenty dollars, the right of trial by jury shall be preserved, and no fact tried by a jury, shall be otherwise re-examined in any Court of the United States, than according to the rules of the common law.

Amendment 8 - Cruel and Unusual Punishment. Ratified 12/15/1791.

Excessive bail shall not be required, nor excessive fines imposed, nor cruel and unusual punishments inflicted.

Amendment 9 - Construction of Constitution. Ratified 12/15/1791.

The enumeration in the Constitution, of certain rights, shall not be construed to deny or disparage others retained by the people.

Amendment 10 - Powers of the States and People. Ratified 12/15/1791.

The powers not delegated to the United States by the Constitution, nor prohibited by it to the States, are reserved to the States respectively, or to the people.

Amendment 11 - Judicial Limits. Ratified 2/7/1795.

The Judicial power of the United States shall not be construed to extend to any suit in law or equity, commenced or prosecuted against one of the United States by Citizens of another State, or by Citizens or Subjects of any Foreign State.

Amendment 12 - Choosing the President, Vice-President. Ratified 6/15/1804.

The Electors shall meet in their respective states, and vote by ballot for President and Vice-President, one of whom, at least, shall not be an inhabitant of the same state with themselves; they shall name in their ballots the person voted for as President, and in distinct ballots the person voted for as Vice-President, and they shall make distinct lists of all persons voted for as President, and of all persons voted for as Vice-President and of the number of votes for each, which lists they shall sign and certify, and transmit sealed to the seat of the government of the United States, directed to the President of the Senate;

The President of the Senate shall, in the presence of the Senate and House of Representatives, open all the certificates and the votes shall then be counted;

The person having the greatest Number of votes for President, shall be the President, if such number be a majority of the whole number of Electors appointed; and if no person have such majority, then from the persons having the highest numbers not exceeding three on the list of those voted for as President, the House of Representatives shall choose immediately, by ballot, the President. But in choosing the President, the votes shall be taken by states, the representation from each state having one vote; a quorum for this purpose shall consist of a member or members from two-thirds of the states, and a majority of all the states shall be necessary to a choice. And if the House of Representatives shall not choose a President whenever the right of choice shall devolve upon them, before the fourth day of March next following, then the Vice-President shall act as President, as in the case of the death or other constitutional disability of the President.

The person having the greatest number of votes as Vice-President, shall be the Vice-President, if such number be a majority of the whole number of Electors appointed, and if no person have a majority, then from the two highest numbers on the list, the Senate shall choose the Vice-President; a quorum for the purpose shall consist of two-thirds of the whole number of Senators, and a majority of the whole number shall be necessary to a choice. But no person constitutionally ineligible to the office of President shall be eligible to that of Vice-President of the United States.

Amendment 13 - Slavery Abolished. Ratified 12/6/1865.

1. Neither slavery nor involuntary servitude, except as a punishment for crime whereof the party shall have been duly convicted, shall exist within the United States, or any place subject to their jurisdiction.

2. Congress shall have power to enforce this article by appropriate legislation.

Amendment 14 - Citizenship Rights. Ratified 7/9/1868.

1. All persons born or naturalized in the United States, and subject to the jurisdiction thereof, are citizens of the United States and of the State wherein they reside. No State shall make or enforce any law which shall abridge the privileges or immunities of citizens of the United States; nor shall any State deprive any person of life, liberty, or property, without due process of law; nor deny to any person within its jurisdiction the equal protection of the laws.

2. Representatives shall be apportioned among the several States according to their respective numbers, counting the whole number of persons in each State, excluding Indians not taxed. But when the right to vote at any election for the choice of electors for President and Vice-President of the United States, Representatives in Congress, the Executive and Judicial officers of a State, or the members of the Legislature thereof, is denied to any of the male inhabitants of such State, being twenty-one years of age, and citizens of the United States, or in any way abridged, except for participation in rebellion, or other crime, the basis of representation therein shall be reduced in the proportion which the number of such male citizens shall bear to the whole number of male citizens twenty-one years of age in such State.

3. No person shall be a Senator or Representative in Congress, or elector of President and Vice-President, or hold any office, civil or military, under the United States, or under any State, who, having previously taken an oath, as a member of Congress, or as an officer of the United States, or as a member of any State legislature, or as an executive or judicial officer of any State, to support the Constitution of the United States, shall have engaged in insurrection or rebellion against the same, or given aid or comfort to the enemies thereof. But Congress may by a vote of two-thirds of each House, remove such disability.

4. The validity of the public debt of the United States, authorized by law, including debts incurred for payment of pensions and bounties for services in suppressing insurrection or rebellion, shall not be questioned. But neither the United States nor any State shall assume or pay any debt or obligation incurred in aid of insurrection or rebellion against the United States, or any claim for the loss or emancipation of any slave; but all such debts, obligations and claims shall be held illegal and void.

5. The Congress shall have power to enforce, by appropriate legislation, the provisions of this article.

Amendment 15 - Race No Bar to Vote. Ratified 2/3/1870.

1. The right of citizens of the United States to vote shall not be denied or abridged by the United States or by any State on account of race, color, or previous condition of servitude.

2. The Congress shall have power to enforce this article by appropriate legislation.

Amendment 16 - Status of Income Tax Clarified. Ratified 2/3/1913.

The Congress shall have power to lay and collect taxes on incomes, from whatever source derived, without apportionment among the several States, and without regard to any census or enumeration.

Amendment 17 - Senators Elected by Popular Vote. Ratified 4/8/1913.

The Senate of the United States shall be composed of two Senators from each State, elected by the people thereof, for six years; and each Senator shall have one vote. The electors in each State shall have the qualifications requisite for electors of the most numerous branch of the State legislatures.

When vacancies happen in the representation of any State in the Senate, the executive authority of such State shall issue writs of election to fill such vacancies: Provided, That the legislature of any State may empower the executive thereof to make temporary appointments until the people fill the vacancies by election as the legislature may direct.

This amendment shall not be so construed as to affect the election or term of any Senator chosen before it becomes valid as part of the Constitution.

Amendment 18 - Liquor Abolished. Ratified 1/16/1919. Repealed by Amendment 21, 12/5/1933.

1. After one year from the ratification of this article the manufacture, sale, or transportation of intoxicating liquors within, the importation thereof into, or the exportation thereof from the United States and all territory subject to the jurisdiction thereof for beverage purposes is hereby prohibited.

2. The Congress and the several States shall have concurrent power to enforce this article by appropriate legislation.

3. This article shall be inoperative unless it shall have been ratified as an amendment to the Constitution by the legislatures of the several States, as

provided in the Constitution, within seven years from the date of the submission hereof to the States by the Congress.

Amendment 19 - Women's Suffrage. Ratified 8/18/1920.

The right of citizens of the United States to vote shall not be denied or abridged by the United States or by any State on account of sex.

Congress shall have power to enforce this article by appropriate legislation.

Amendment 20 - Presidential, Congressional Terms. Ratified 1/23/1933.

1. The terms of the President and Vice President shall end at noon on the 20th day of January, and the terms of Senators and Representatives at noon on the 3d day of January, of the years in which such terms would have ended if this article had not been ratified; and the terms of their successors shall then begin.

2. The Congress shall assemble at least once in every year, and such meeting shall begin at noon on the 3d day of January, unless they shall by law appoint a different day.

3. If, at the time fixed for the beginning of the term of the President, the President elect shall have died, the Vice President elect shall become President. If a President shall not have been chosen before the time fixed for the beginning of his term, or if the President elect shall have failed to qualify, then the Vice President elect shall act as President until a President shall have qualified; and the Congress may by law provide for the case wherein neither a President elect nor a Vice President elect shall have qualified, declaring who shall then act as President, or the manner in which one who is to act shall be selected, and such person shall act accordingly until a President or Vice President shall have qualified.

4. The Congress may by law provide for the case of the death of any of the persons from whom the House of Representatives may choose a President whenever the right of choice shall have devolved upon them, and for the case of the death of any of the persons from whom the Senate may choose a Vice President whenever the right of choice shall have devolved upon them.

5. Sections 1 and 2 shall take effect on the 15th day of October following the ratification of this article.

6. This article shall be inoperative unless it shall have been ratified as an amendment to the Constitution by the legislatures of three-fourths of the several States within seven years from the date of its submission.

Amendment 21 - Amendment 18 Repealed. Ratified 12/5/1933.

1. The eighteenth article of amendment to the Constitution of the United States is hereby repealed.

2. The transportation or importation into any State, Territory, or possession of the United States for delivery or use therein of intoxicating liquors, in violation of the laws thereof, is hereby prohibited.

3. The article shall be inoperative unless it shall have been ratified as an amendment to the Constitution by conventions in the several States, as provided in the Constitution, within seven years from the date of the submission hereof to the States by the Congress.

Amendment 22 - Presidential Term Limits. Ratified 2/27/1951.

1. No person shall be elected to the office of the President more than twice, and no person who has held the office of President, or acted as President, for more than two years of a term to which some other person was elected President shall be elected to the office of the President more than once. But this Article shall not apply to any person holding the office of President, when this Article was proposed by the Congress, and shall not prevent any person who may be holding the office of President, or acting as President, during the term within which this Article becomes operative from holding the office of President or acting as President during the remainder of such term.

2. This article shall be inoperative unless it shall have been ratified as an amendment to the Constitution by the legislatures of three-fourths of the several States within seven years from the date of its submission to the States by the Congress.

Amendment 23 - Presidential Vote for District of Columbia. Ratified 3/29/1961.

1. The District constituting the seat of Government of the United States shall appoint in such manner as the Congress may direct: A number of electors of President and Vice President equal to the whole number of Senators and Representatives in Congress to which the District would be entitled if it were a State, but in no event more than the least populous State; they shall be in addition to those appointed by the States, but they shall be considered, for the purposes of the election of President and Vice President, to be electors appointed by a State; and they shall meet in the District and perform such duties as provided by the twelfth article of amendment.

2. The Congress shall have power to enforce this article by appropriate legislation.

Amendment 24 - Poll Tax Barred. Ratified 1/23/1964.

1. The right of citizens of the United States to vote in any primary or other election for President or Vice President, for electors for President or Vice President, or for Senator or Representative in Congress, shall not be denied or abridged by the United States or any State by reason of failure to pay any poll tax or other tax.

2. The Congress shall have power to enforce this article by appropriate legislation.

Amendment 25 - Presidential Disability and Succession. Ratified 2/10/1967.

1. In case of the removal of the President from office or of his death or resignation, the Vice President shall become President.

2. Whenever there is a vacancy in the office of the Vice President, the President shall nominate a Vice President who shall take office upon confirmation by a majority vote of both Houses of Congress.

3. Whenever the President transmits to the President pro tempore of the Senate and the Speaker of the House of Representatives his written declaration that he is unable to discharge the powers and duties of his office, and until he transmits to them a written declaration to the contrary, such powers and duties shall be discharged by the Vice President as Acting President.

4. Whenever the Vice President and a majority of either the principal officers of the executive departments or of such other body as Congress may by law provide, transmit to the President pro tempore of the Senate and the Speaker of the House of Representatives their written declaration that the President is unable to discharge the powers and duties of his office, the Vice President shall immediately assume the powers and duties of the office as Acting President.

Thereafter, when the President transmits to the President pro tempore of the Senate and the Speaker of the House of Representatives his written declaration that no inability exists, he shall resume the powers and duties of his office unless the Vice President and a majority of either the principal officers of the executive department or of such other body as Congress may by law provide, transmit within four days to the President pro tempore of the Senate and the Speaker of the House of Representatives their written declaration that the President is unable to discharge the powers and duties of his office. Thereupon Congress shall decide the issue, assembling within forty eight hours for that purpose if not in session. If the Congress, within twenty one days after receipt of the latter written declaration, or, if Congress is not in session, within twenty one days after Congress is required to assemble, determines by two thirds vote of both Houses that the President is unable to discharge the powers and duties of his office, the Vice President shall continue to discharge the same as Acting President; otherwise, the President shall resume the powers and duties of his office.

Amendment 26 - Voting Age Set to 18 Years. Ratified 7/1/1971.

1. The right of citizens of the United States, who are eighteen years of age or older, to vote shall not be denied or abridged by the United States or by any State on account of age.

2. The Congress shall have power to enforce this article by appropriate legislation.

Amendment 27 - Limiting Changes to Congressional Pay. Ratified 5/7/1992.

No law, varying the compensation for the services of the Senators and Representatives, shall take effect, until an election of Representatives shall have intervened.

34912389R00103

Made in the USA
Middletown, DE
10 September 2016